pathfinder guide

D0018350

Cornwall

W A L K S

Compiled by
John Brooks

JARROLD

Ordnance Survey

Acknowledgements
We would like to thank James MacFarlane and Richard
Horwood of Cornwall County Council for reading the
manuscript and checking the maps.
Thanks also to Mr A.J. Collins, Mr B and Mrs H Gilbert, and
Mrs J Allgood who kindly supplied information used to
update the text for this reprint.

Text:	John Brooks
Photography:	John Brooks, Jarrold Publishing
Editors:	Thomas Albrighton, Donald Greig
Designers:	Brian Skinner, Doug Whitworth
Mapping:	Heather Pearson, Sandy Sims

Series Consultant: Brian Conduit

© Jarrold Publishing and Ordnance Survey 1990, 1996, 1998
Maps © Crown copyright 1996. The mapping in this guide is
based upon Ordnance Survey ® Pathfinder ®, Outdoor Leisure ™,
Explorer ™ and Travelmaster ® mapping.
Ordnance Survey, Pathfinder and Travelmaster are registered
trade marks and Outdoor Leisure and Explorer are trade marks of
Ordnance Survey, the National Mapping Agency of Great Britain.

Jarrold Publishing   ISBN 0-7117-0457-0

First published 1990
by Jarrold Publishing and Ordnance Survey
Reprinted 1991, 1993, 1996, 1998

Printed in Great Britain
by Jarrold Book Printing, Thetford 5/98

Jarrold Publishing,
Whitefriars, Norwich NR3 1TR
Ordnance Survey,
Romsey Road, Southampton SO16 4GU

Front cover:	Land's End
Previous page:	St Ives

Contents

■ Short, easy walks

■ Walks of modest length, likely to involve some modest uphill walking

■ More challenging walks which may be longer and/or over more rugged terrain, often with some stiff climbs

Keymap 1

SCALE 1:250 000 or 1 INCH to 4 MILES *1CM to 2.5KM*

Keymap 1

Keymap 2

SCALE 1:250 000 or 1 INCH to 4 MILES *1CM to 2.5KM*

KILOMETRES

MILES

At-a-glance...

Walk	Page	Start	Distance	Time
Chûn Quoit, Pendeen Watch and Botallack	60	Carnyorth	8 miles (12.75km)	4½ hrs
Dizzard Point, St Gennys and Millook Water	64	Cancleave	7 miles (11.25km)	4½ hrs
The Dodman, Gorran Haven and Portmellon	86	Caerhays Beach	11 miles (17.5km)	6 hrs
Efford Down and the Bude Canal	28	Bude	5 miles (8km)	3 hrs
Falmouth Bay and the Helford River	34	Maenporth Beach	5 miles (8km)	2½ hrs
Hawker Country – Morwenstow and Marsland Mouth	38	Morwenstow	4½ miles (7.25km)	3 hrs
Helford, Little Dennis and Manaccan	36	Helford	5 miles (8km)	2½ hrs
Lamorna, St Loy's and the Merry Maidens	78	Lamorna Cove	8½ miles (13.5km)	4 hrs
Land's End and Nanjizal from Sennen	41	Sennen harbour	5½ miles (8.75km)	3 hrs
Lerryn and St Winnow	14	Lerryn	5 miles (8km)	3 hrs
Little Petherick Creek, Dennis Hill and the Camel Trail	54	Little Petherick	6 miles (9.5km)	3 hrs
Lizard Point, Kynance Cove and Cadgwith	67	Lizard Point	8 miles (12.75km)	4 hrs
Looe, Kilminorth Wood and Talland Bay	46	Entrance to Kilminorth Wood, West Looe	7 miles (11.25km)	3½ hrs
Mên-an-tol, the Nine Maidens and Lanyon Quoit	16	Bosullow	4½ miles (7.25km)	2 hrs
Mount Edgcumbe, the Sound and Cawsand	43	Cremyll	6 miles (9.5km)	3 hrs
Mylor, Restronguet Creek and the Pandora Inn	20	Mylor Bridge	5 miles (8km)	3 hrs
Polkerris, Readymoney Cove and Gribbin Head	51	Polkerris	6½ miles (10.5km)	3 hrs
Polruan and Lanteglos	22	Polruan	4 miles (6.5km)	2½ hrs
Porthcurno, Porthgwarra and St Levan's Church	26	Porthcurno	4 miles (6.5km)	2½ hrs
Portloe and Veryan	57	Carne Beach, near Veryan	7 miles (11.25km)	4 hrs
Prussia Cove and Cudden Point	24	Perranuthnoe	4½ miles (7.25km)	3 hrs
Around St Agnes	49	Trevaunance Cove, St Agnes	5½ miles (8.75km)	3 hrs
St Anthony Head and St Mawes Harbour	30	Porth Farm	6 miles (9.5km)	3 hrs
Stepper Point from Trevone	32	Trevone Bay	7 miles (11.25km)	3 hrs
Tintagel, Boscastle and St Nectan's Glen	82	Tintagel	9 miles (14.5km)	5 hrs
Trebarwith and Delabole	74	Trebarwith Strand	9 miles (14.5km)	5½ hrs
West Pentire, the Kelseys and Holywell Bay	18	West Pentire	5 miles (8km)	2½ hrs
Zennor to St Ives by the Tinners' Way	71	Zennor	8½ miles (13.5km)	4½ hrs

Comments

The far west of Cornwall has a unique character of landscape. This route explores interesting aspects of history and scenery, visiting the finest of the Cornish quoits as well as the most romantic mine.

Avoid this walk if bad weather is in the offing as much of it is along high exposed cliffs. Be warned too that there is a fair amount of climbing involved, though the landscapes are wild and beautiful.

If you added up the total height climbed on this route it would probably be the equivalent of a Lake District mountain. The coastal section is magnificent and the countryside return no anti-climax.

North Cornwall is one of the last places where one would expect to find a canal, but the one at Bude is fascinating and is a perfect complement to the cliff walk which forms the outward leg.

The chief pleasure in this walk lies in the way that the route alternates between woodland and open countryside. Rosemullion Head is a grand viewpoint for a panorama of Falmouth Bay.

There are many sailors' graves in the churchyard at Morwenstow for in the days of sail this was a perilous coastline. You can appreciate this on the way back on the coastal path along the clifftop.

The outward part of the route is along the wooded shoreline of the Helford River to Dennis Head. The return follows Gillan Creek before striking inland. Note that dogs are not allowed.

Energetic scrambling over boulders is necessary at the beginning and end, in a walk which explores the coastal and inland landscape of the Land's End peninsula. A shorter alternative is suggested.

You can visit Land's End without paying by following this route. There are crowds near the car park, but a little distance away all is peace and beauty and this walk takes you to the best of the scenery.

Lerryn is a famous beauty-spot half-hidden by the tortuous course of the River Fowey. The walk is by the river as well as through woods and over fields, the latter giving wide views.

The Saints' Way crosses Cornwall from north to south and this route makes use of the long-distance footpath and also follows the Camel Trail along a disused railway which once went to Padstow.

The walk takes you to the most spectacular part of the Lizard peninsula and starts from Lizard Point itself, visiting Kynance Cove and passing close to the lovely fishing village of Cadgwith.

At first the way lies through woodland on the side of a creek, but later there are stretches along farm tracks before the return on the coast path. This makes an enjoyable and undemanding ramble.

This short walk takes you to some of West Cornwall's most famous prehistoric monuments. It also gives you the opportunity of appreciating the unique beauty of the Penwith peninsula.

Easternmost Cornwall remains a mystery to many visitors but this neglect is unfair, as shown by this walk, much of which falls within the Mount Edgcumbe estate. There are also views of Plymouth Sound.

Try to walk this route at high tide as this shows the natural beauty of the estuary at its best. The picturesque Pandora Inn comes at the halfway point just when refreshments are most welcome.

Here you explore the coastal landscape loved by Daphne du Maurier, author of *Jamaica Inn*. The walk encircles the estate where she lived and its inland section is as much fun as the earlier, seaside, one.

Polruan is a delightful little place which looks over the wide estuary to Fowey. The walk gives a succession of vistas of river and coastline and is a favourite with locals and visitors alike.

A wonderful variety of scenery is packed into a short distance here. There is a very steep climb at the start up the cliffs which give the Minack Theatre its incomparable backdrop.

This is a perfect family walk, though the opening clifftop section will prove taxing to those unused to walking. It is followed by a delightful inland section on lanes and field paths back to Veryan.

The outward leg of this route is over field paths and tracks which wind through fertile agricultural land. The return is via the coast path visiting romantic Prussia Cove and giving superb views of Mount's Bay.

Although this is a short walk it requires a good deal of energy, especially if you decide to climb St Agnes Beacon - very worthwhile on a clear day. The final part of the walk is by a delightful stream.

Clifftop and creekside walking combine here in an excellent circuit through varied and often wooded scenery. Birdwatchers will have the opportunity of spotting seabirds, waders, and woodland species. .

You may well feel that the best part of this walk is the beginning, on the springy clifftop turf heading for Stepper Point. The return is less spectacular but still enjoyable, with a visit to Padstow optional.

Tintagel claims to be Cornwall's most romantic village and here you go past its famous castle to reach precipitous cliffs. You also visit Boscastle and St Nectan's Glen, a tourist attraction of yesteryear.

There are two versions of this walk but in both the demanding clifftop section comes first. The return leg is via field paths where some skill and common sense will be needed for navigation.

This is a delightfully varied walk which is entirely on footpaths. They take you over the springy turf of Cubert Common, the sandy dunes of the Kelseys, and along the cliffs of Pentire Point.

The inland part of this route follows the old Coffin Path from farm to farm which is hardly less fun than the exciting return along the coastal path on the cliff edge. Note that there is a shorter alternative route.

At-a-glance...

Introduction to Cornwall

The Duchy of Cornwall is the far west of England, dipping a toe into the Atlantic as though gingerly testing its waters for warmth. Both its history and landscape are romantic, and as in many areas with such scenery, its people have suffered because of the beauty that surrounded them, for the land was always hard to till while the riches of the coastal waters were never dependable and have always been difficult to harvest with the rocky shore merciless.

It is a sad aspect of the history of Cornwall that its natural resources have often failed with dramatic suddenness. Tin-mining ended abruptly in the early nineteenth century when it became possible to import the ore more cheaply from abroad rather than win it from the county's dangerously deep mines. Many of the old engine-houses of the industry remain as a glorious characteristic of the Cornish landscape.

Similarly, another of Cornwall's legendary riches vanished almost overnight. At the turn of the century fishermen depended on shoals of pilchards appearing off the coast regularly each summer. For no obvious reason the shoals suddenly ceased to visit Cornish waters, and the fishermen were forced to turn to other fish for their livelihoods, less easily won from the deep.

Apart from the picturesque 'Huers' Houses' still to be seen at St Ives and Newquay, nothing remains to remind us of this abrupt change of fortune that hit Cornish fishing ports in the early years of this century. Fortunately there was compensation in the growth of the tourist industry, which had begun with the arrival of the Great Western Railway 50 years before. This industry showed another dramatic increase after World War II, when the private car became essential to every family. More recently the building of the M5 motorway boosted tourism again, and today much the greatest part of Cornwall's prosperity depends on holiday visitors.

Several factors contribute to Cornwall's popularity as a holiday venue. Firstly, its climate usually provides more sunshine and warmth than elsewhere in Britain (though to be honest, there is also a likelihood of more rain). Secondly, for those who enjoy traditional British holidaying, there are innumerable sun-drenched beaches of more-or-less blemish-free sand. Most also have an abundance of rock pools which young children delight in exploring. Some may despair of the commercialism which often accompanies such scenic beauty, but few families can fail to enjoy the natural amenities, especially when bathing is safe, or at any rate supervised. The third reason for the Duchy's popularity concerns us more directly here. This is Cornwall's superlative all-round natural beauty which is too often ignored by holiday visitors. Its magnificent coastal path gives access to many of Britain's finest marine landscapes: a great many of the walks contained in this book utilise sections of this path. It is to Cornwall's everlasting credit that the path has been created and is maintained to such a high standard.

Caerhays

Inevitably the same does not hold true for all of the Duchy's footpaths. By their very nature footpaths were not intended to take the user in a circle. In Cornwall they often linked farms to hamlets and hamlets to villages, or they were the paths used by miners or fishermen. Thus it is not always as easy as it might seem to make up circular routes that provide both interest and beauty. Many of the rights of way marked on definitive maps have become choked up through disuse, simply because people prefer to use the excellent coastal route rather than one that winds through the fields a mile or so (1.5km) inland. There are no paths in this book which will be found to be impassable, though one or two may need a touch of pioneering spirit.

An unfortunate deficiency that will be noticed is the lack of any walks on Bodmin Moor. Like Dartmoor in the neighbouring county, the landscape of Bodmin Moor is important to anyone interested in the physical and historical development of Cornwall. The wild moor is a natural landscape untamed by man and thus is unique in this area, apart from the uplands of West Penwith. Unhappily, although walkers may enjoy exploring the moor and are unlikely to be turned off any of the marked tracks as long as they are obeying the Country Code, they will very often be trespassing. Right-of-way footpaths are few and far between and quite often end in the middle of nowhere. Landowners, the Duchy of Cornwall notable amongst them, do not welcome guidebooks suggesting routes that enter private land, and thus we cannot include any here, which is regrettable since the walking to places such as the Cheesewring is so enjoyable. Caradon District Council has had a Minions Project in the pipeline for some years now which would allow legal access to the Cheesewring, but negotiations with the Duchy seem to be deadlocked at the moment. This is a great shame as this is one of Cornwall's finest viewpoints set amidst a wealth of antiquities, and good signposting would keep people from wandering off the authorised paths and tracks. It seems sad that such a rare tract of truly wild country as the moor is not more open to walkers. Access to it might ease the pressure on other, overburdened, paths, such as parts of the coastal path and Dartmoor.

Bodmin Moor is a landscape which has altered little since the first settlers came to Cornwall early in the Iron Age, nearly 3000 years ago. These people left monuments here, but little else. Further west, however, more useful evidence of their presence survives, and is shown on the maps. Look at the small fields which surround Zennor: many of these date from this time, their stone walls (known here as hedges) being distinctively built with massive boulders at the base, and smaller stones on top. In contrast, the long, narrow fields of north-east Cornwall are of Anglo-Saxon date, as are many of the enclosed, sunken lanes and paths which connect them, wandering across the countryside in what seems a haphazard fashion today, but which once responded to local needs.

Although the coastal path is Cornwall's best-known long-distance footpath, there are two others that deserve to be walked more frequently. The Saints' Way crosses Cornwall from coast to coast, following a route pioneered by the early Christian missionaries and by merchants wishing to avoid the perilous voyage round Land's End. The path starts at Padstow and ends at Fowey, passing through some of the loveliest of Cornwall's inland countryside. Two of the routes in this book follow it for a short distance – Walk 18 on the south coast, and Walk 19 which follows the route near Padstow. The other named path is the Tinners' Way, which follows a complicated course through the old tin workings of the Penwith district of west Cornwall. Walks 21 and 24 include sections of this interesting and historic route.

Practical considerations

Cornwall is a delight at any time of the year, but there can be no denying that spring paints it most richly. Daffodils and bluebells bloom on cliffs which appear barren at other times. The lanes glow with early wild flowers, and for a week or so the trees take on almost autumnal colour before the buds burst and the leaves show their wonderful fresh green. In late April and early May the days are lengthening and growing warmer – yet not too warm for walking. Summer sees Cornwall at its busiest, yet though the beaches may be thronged there are seldom more than a handful of people on the footpaths. The days are long and warm, and it seems easy to cover fifteen or even twenty miles in a day. Foxgloves and gorse provide contrasting colour, while the sea has the brilliance found only in the far west. Although it may be tempting to wear a minimum of clothing, shorts can prove to be a mistake when brambles, nettles or gorse are encountered.

The Cheesewring, Bodmin Moor

Take account of the weather forecast and if there is any hint of rain be sure to take waterproofs. Remember, too, that though it may be warm in a sheltered car park it can be freezing on an exposed clifftop.

In autumn, although the days draw in there is still time for good walking. Where there are trees the colours can be spectacular, as can the effects wrought by a low sun on the seascapes. In this season weather has an importance not appreciated before, and routes have to be chosen that take this into account. There is little pleasure in having to walk six or seven miles on an open clifftop in the face of an Atlantic gale, though the vista of boiling surf may make less ambitious expeditions memorable.

This is even more true in winter, of course, but there are still days when walking is fun, especially if the route is carefully selected. Mud can be a problem at any time of the year, and even in high summer boots are recommended for most of these walks; in winter they are essential. Also remember that after the month of September most of the cafés and quite a few of the pubs will be closed, so be sure to take emergency rations and give yourself plenty of spare time: it is no fun finishing a walk in the gloom of December twilight.

The times given in the introductions to the walks are very approximate. All sorts of factors may slow you down: a headwind along a stretch of exposed cliff might add an hour or so to the time taken, and children or dogs can also delay progress. The author can testify that an eight-year-old will cheerfully walk (and talk) for six or so hours on even the more taxing of these routes, and there is only one instance (Walk 12, Helford) where dogs are forbidden. However, dogs should always be kept under control, especially in the lambing and nesting season.

Lerryn and St Winnow

Start	Lerryn, south of Lostwithiel
Distance	5 miles (8km) Shorter version 2 miles (3.25km)
Approximate time	3 hours (1 hour for shorter version)
Parking	Car park on the south side of the river at Lerryn
Refreshments	Pub at Lerryn
Ordnance Survey maps	Landranger 200 (Newquay & Bodmin) and Pathfinder 1354, SX 05/15 (St Austell & Fowey)

An easy and very pleasant walk which combines a riverside route through woodland with, on the return leg, a pastoral section which allows more open views of beautiful, rolling countryside. The walk can be shortened, if wished, after point ❹ below.

It is best to visit Lerryn with the tide up, for then it is at its most picturesque (though an exceptionally high tide could make parts of the walk difficult, especially the start and at St Winnow). Having left the car park, cross the bridge and take the lane to the left to find the riverside path. This soon enters the National Trust's Ethy Woods, the path following the course of the creek and reaching the head of the first inlet (or pill) at ❹.

At this point, those wishing only to do the shorter version of the walk can bear to the right at the footpath

Lerryn

junction here. This path leads up the valley past Nott's Mill to rejoin the route at ruined St Winnow Mill.

Continue through shady woodland, the path climbing to reach a track which becomes an avenue through broom bushes, fragrant in early summer. However the footpath soon bears left off this track to follow the course of the creek again and skirt Mendy Pill.

In summer the trees screen views of the creek. The path bends almost imperceptibly around St Winnow Point, the southernmost extent of the walk. On the right plantings of conifers herald the end of the woodland section. The wood thins out and a stile leads into a meadow. The ancient grey tower of St Winnow Church comes into view. If the tide is out it is easy to follow the path along the foreshore and into the churchyard. A high tide may make a diversion necessary.

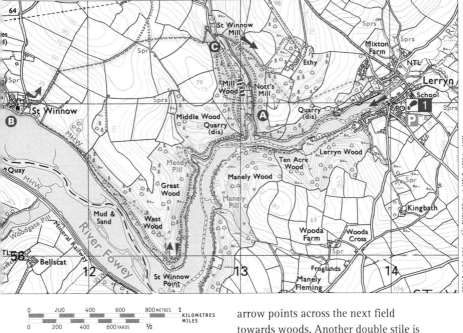

```
0    2U0   400   600   800 METRES  1
                                      KILOMETRES
                                      MILES
0    200   400   600 YARDS  ½
```

The church **B**, some of its fabric dating from Norman times, has much to offer besides its wonderful location (a favourite with film-makers). There is some lovely 16th-century glass in the west window and one of the bench ends shows a medieval Cornishman swigging from a quart pot. St Winnow also has an interesting farming museum displaying implements of bygone days.

The footpath turns to the right before the museum, passing through a gate and then following a farm track with an orchard on the right. It climbs steeply uphill, passing through a second gate. There are good views back to the River Fowey.

Bear right at the top, following the yellow waymark to cross the field diagonally. Then cross a double stile into the next field and keep the bank on the left. The view back from here is even more beautiful than previously. In the following field bear to the right to cross it to a gate and stile in the middle of the hedge on the right. Here a yellow arrow points across the next field towards woods. Another double stile is reached. Climb this and continue down the hill towards the trees keeping the hedge on the left, looking for a stile on the left before the woods. Cross this and now keep the hedge on the right descending the hill to find a stile on the right giving on to a lane. Turn right here down the lane to pass the ruins of St Winnow Mill and cross its stream. The track climbs away from the mill to meet another footpath from the right (from Nott's Mill) at the start of the woods **C**.

Turn left here up a steep hill; keep to the top path. Climb the stile at the top and cross the field. The path here passes to the right of an enormous oak tree to reach a gateway. Pass through this and now keep the bank (and the handsome mansion of Ethy) on the left as you descend to a stile incorporating an ingenious dog-gate. The path continues downhill to a similar stile to the right of the bungalows by the far right-hand corner of the field. Turn left at the head of the cul-de-sac, then right down the lane leading back to the riverside path and the bridge at Lerryn. ●

Mên-an-tol, the Nine Maidens and Lanyon Quoit

Start	Bosullow
Distance	4½ miles (7.25km) Shorter version 3 miles (4.75km)
Approximate time	2 hours (1½ hours for shorter version)
Parking	Bosullow, opposite Mên-an-Tol Studio, on the Penzance to Morvah road
Refreshments	None
Ordnance Survey maps	Landranger 203 (Land's End) and Explorer 7 (Land's End)

If you are interested only in off-the-road walking, then you may well prefer the shorter route (which you can take just after point **D** *below), for the longer one which visits Lanyon Quoit entails a distance along the road. The walking is easy, very reminiscent of Bodmin Moor or Dartmoor, and includes splendid views over Mount's Bay. There is also the bonus of seeing a different sort of antiquity of the far west – the famous Ding Dong Mine, as well as the Mên-an-tol, the Nine Maidens, and Mên Scryfa.*

Start at the footpath signpost to Mên-an-tol and Mên Scryfa nearly opposite the telephone box. The path is easy and makes enjoyable walking. After about 15 minutes a sign on the right points to a path through the heather and gorse to the famous monument of Mên-an-tol **A**, a large stone with a hole in it large enough for a child to pass through. Though its prehistoric significance is unknown, it was popular in more recent centuries for its magical powers: for instance it was believed that children suffering from rickets could be cured by passing through the centre of the stone.

It is best to return to the main track after examining the stone, partly because Mên Scryfa, a famous inscribed stone, lies to its left a short distance on (look for a stone stile on the left and a standing stone in a field in front of a rocky tor), and also because the path going directly to Ding Dong (the engine house on the skyline) is overgrown by prickly gorse.

It is hard to see anything inscribed on Mên Scryfa, though there does appear to be some sort of a pattern on its far side. From its field, return again to the main track.

Pass the sad remains of a ruined cottage **B** on the left and head up towards the summit of the hill (don't turn right towards the ruined engine-house of Ding Dong, 'the oldest and most romantic deserted mine in the country' according to an old guidebook). Our path leads to the Nine Maidens  C – a Bronze Age stone circle which once had twenty-two stones – before twisting through the heather to Ding Dong D. As the old engine-house of the famous mine is approached the view on the left opens up to give a spectacular panorama of Mount's Bay.

If you choose the shorter version of the walk, descend to a rutted track on the south-west side of the engine-house, passing through an old iron gate. Follow this downhill with the radio mast ahead to reach the road near Lanyon Farm. Turn right to return to the starting point.

Mên-an-tol

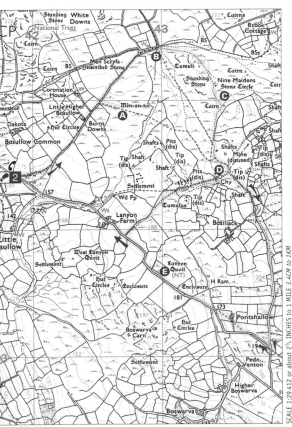

From Ding Dong take the track which leads past an underground reservoir. Every now and then climb the bank on the left side of the lane to look out over a typically Cornish landscape of small fields and abandoned mines. Pass the drive to Bosiliack Farm on the right and come on to a made-up lane. Turn right when this meets a major lane. After this road twists left and begins to descend take a short-cut using a stone stile on top of the bank on the right. This crosses fields in front of Pontshallow. Lanyon Quoit E can soon be seen on the right. One of the Penwith group of gallery graves, it possibly dates from 2000 BC. It was restored in the 19th century.

From Lanyon follow the lane back to the starting point. ●

West Pentire, the Kelseys and Holywell Bay

Start	West Pentire, west of Crantock near Newquay
Distance	5 miles (8km)
Approximate time	2½ hours
Parking	West Pentire car park (pay and display)
Refreshments	Hotel at West Pentire, cafés and pubs at Holywell Bay
Ordnance Survey maps	Landranger 200 (Newquay & Bodmin) and Pathfinder 1352, SW 75 (Perranporth)

A delightfully varied walk which also has the advantage of being confined entirely to footpaths. The inland stretch covers the springy turf of Cubert Common and the sand dunes of the Kelseys, while the clifftop walk gives superb vistas both near and far. It is not difficult to include Newquay on the route (or start from there) by using the Crantock Ferry.

Turn left out of the West Pentire car park and walk down a farm track which winds through a strange sandy landscape of rolling dunes. This soon descends steeply to a valley. Turn to the right at the gateway to Treago Mill Ⓐ and cross a stream by the footbridge. Turn right after the kissing-gate by Porth Joke camping site and then bear left to follow the valley southwards. Turn right before the white cottage at the top of the hill Ⓑ (beware of friendly horses here which chew cameras). Cross the head of the valley and climb the hill in front (this is a grassy track, not the one that follows the wall on left). Stride along on lovely springy turf to reach an ancient bank with a fence on top. Keep this on the right until you reach the National Trust gateway into the Kelseys.

The Kelseys is a unique area protected by plantings of marram and fences designed to keep people away from the easily-eroded dunes. The keen-eyed will spot many unusual plants and insects. Rabbits abound on the edges of the Kelseys.

After the National Trust sign keep the wall on the left and pass through two kissing-gates to reach the path through the dunes. In summer you will find sea holly and sea bindweed in bloom and hear the music made by a hundred grasshoppers. Continue with the fence and golf course on the left until at the bottom of the valley you are confronted with a 'Private Keep Out' notice-board. Turn to the right here Ⓒ along a well defined path which leads to a track passing in front of bungalows. Leave this on the left as soon as possible turning towards the sea without crossing the fence on the right erected to protect the dunes. Should you feel like finding refreshment at a pub, continue into Holywell village, keeping the bungalows on your left.

Continuing over the dunes, a beach café can soon be seen on the left. Now keep the fence on the right and the stream on the left, and follow the path over the dunes to the sea, using the wooden track laid down to help the life-savers' Land Rover. It makes a change to walk along the beach for ¼ mile (400m) or so here. The twin rocks offshore are the Gull Rocks, and the southern headland Penhale Point. There is a legend which says that the fabulous city of Langarroc lies under the great expanse of dunes which stretch from Penhale to Perranporth, which was drowned in sand as a judgement on the wickedness of its inhabitants.

Look for timber steps climbing the marram shortly before the dunes give way to rocky cliffs. A kissing-gate **D** marks the abrupt change between sand-dunes and clifftop meadow. A second gate leads out on to Kelsey Head. From here to Porth Joke the scenery is spectacular with distant views of Newquay and Watergate bays. Prolong the enjoyment of the walk by following the twists of the coast rather than cutting across the numerous minor headlands. Note the raised bank of the ancient settlement at Kelsey Head and ponder on why the rock offshore is named The Chick.

Similarly, how did Porth Joke get its name? Apparently it is a corruption of

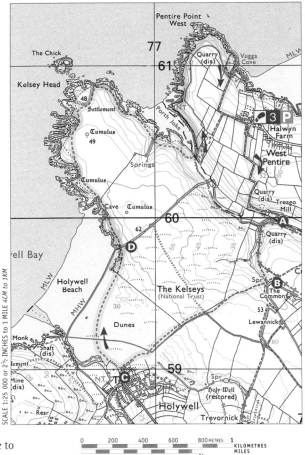

the Cornish 'gwic', meaning a creek. This is a good place to appreciate the tortured strata of Cornwall's bedrock. It is easy to take a short cut across the beach here if the tide allows, scrambling up the rocks on the other of side to regain the cliff path.

Pentire Point West is a favourite haunt of fishermen, with a lovely view of Crantock, the beach and the village. In early times this was the main port of the district, used by travellers from Ireland *en route* to Brittany to avoid the hazardous passage round Land's End.

Leave the coast path just before the stile, turning to the right up a narrow enclosed path. Pass through the gate at the top of this and turn left to return to the car park. ●

Mylor, Restronguet Creek and the Pandora Inn

Start	Mylor Bridge, north of Falmouth
Distance	5 miles (8km)
Approximate time	3 hours
Parking	Public car park opposite Mylor Bridge
Refreshments	Pub at Mylor Bridge and at Restronguet Passage
Ordnance Survey maps	Landranger 204 (Truro & Falmouth) and Pathfinder 1366, SW 83/73/93 (Falmouth & St Mawes)

This is a pleasant stroll for a summer's evening, though the navigation back to Mylor Bridge might become difficult if the food and drink at the Pandora Inn prove too beguiling. The walking is easy and the views of the Carrick Roads and across Restronguet Creek are always interesting, both for their beauty and for the glimpses offered of the splendid creekside houses. As with most creekside walks, it is at its best with the tide up.

Cross the road from the car park to Trevellan Road opposite, which leads past the post office. At the quay follow the footpath sign for Restronguet. The way briefly threads between houses before emerging into a meadow which the path crosses to reach the river again, keeping above the shoreline on the edge of the fields. The riverside trees allow only occasional enticing views of Mylor Creek, where the predominant features are boats and expensive homes. Mylor Churchtown, on the other side of the river, can be seen through the trees after about 20 minutes' walking.

At Greatwood Quay Ⓐ the path changes direction, and from here a magnificent expanse of river can be seen. Subsequently the path climbs to allow even better views. Keep to the right when you meet another footpath coming from Restronguet Barton. Our

path passes behind Greatwood House with its Scots-baronial-style tower.

At Weir Point the path briefly takes to the beach (and not up the road to the left) before following the shoreline along the lane past Beach Cottage. The Pandora Inn Ⓑ at Restronguet Passage, one of the most picturesque West Country pubs and the halfway point of this walk, appears suddenly.

The building, originally a 13th-century farmhouse, became an inn known as the Passage-House since it was the base for the ferry providing a short-cut for road passengers between Falmouth and Truro. In 1791 the ferry sank and several lives were lost; soon after the inn changed its name to The Ship. It was bought by a retired sea captain and renamed after the last ship under his command, HMS *Pandora*, which was sent to Tahiti to capture seamen who mutinied against Captain

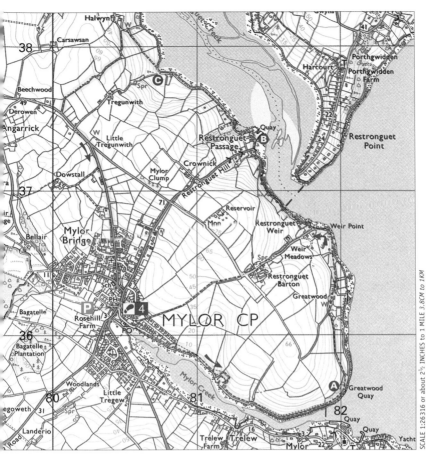

Mylor Creek

Bligh on the *Bounty*, and which struck the Great Barrier Reef and sank, many of the crew being drowned. The captain, named Edwards, was court-martialled on his return and afterwards retired to Cornwall.

Leaving the pub, continue to follow the shore towards Halwyn (signposted). Once past the houses this is a lovely section of the walk, with exotic birds on the mud-flats and honeysuckle in the hedges. The once-splendid trees hardly seem to be thriving, unfortunately. The view opens up in front of a white house, and from here **C** the footpath follows a made-up road which climbs away from the river. Cross three cattle-grids (do not miss the superb views back), and bear sharply to the left before Halwyn along a track which eventually emerges on the lane above Mylor Bridge. Turn left to go down to the village, turning left again in the village itself, and then right immediately to return to the car park. ●

Polruan and Lanteglos

Start	Polruan
Distance	4 miles (6.5km)
Approximate time	2½ hours
Parking	Polruan harbour car park, or upper car park
Refreshments	Pubs and cafés in Polruan
Ordnance Survey maps	Landranger 204 (Truro & Falmouth) and Pathfinder 1354, SX 05/15 (St Austell & Fowey)

Polruan is one of Cornwall's better-kept secrets, and this walk offers the opportunity of seeing its beautiful setting as well. Lanteglos church is also off the beaten track and it too deserves to be better known. This is a short walk but some of the gradients, though not lengthy, are quite severe.

If you have been fortunate enough to park on the quay you will see a footpath sign pointing to the left, to 'The Hills', as you enter the main street of the town. However, if you have left the car in the top car park don't worry, the last part of the walk passes through it, so a climb back is not necessary. Descend to the harbour via Tinker's Hill and turn to the right at the waterfront for the quay. Then follow the signpost straight on for 'The Hills' instead of turning to the left down to the quay. By now you will be aware of the wide choice of refreshments offered here – pubs, cafés, and even a bistro.

The way to The Hills at first follows a narrow lane, then at some steps bears right following the sign on a green-painted house. Climb these steps and then turn to the left at a pink house. Panoramic views of the river open up on the left **Ⓐ** as the path climbs steeply. Strategically-placed seats give one a welcome place to recover and enjoy the view at the same time.

Keep to the top path when it enters trees (there is a National Trust sign

'North Downs'). The trees close in as the path turns to follow the creek below. When it meets a track **Ⓑ** turn right and follow this for 20 yds (18m) before turning left through the trees. Cross a small stream and by a seat keep to the upper path. There are views towards the head of the creek below and a short steep climb to a gate on to the road. Do not go through – keep on a footpath following a National Trust signpost 'Pont and Hall Walk' by turning left.

The path follows the road down, but on the opposite side of the wall. The slope is so steep one wonders how the fields on the left are cultivated. The path is steep too, as it descends to the head of the creek. Bear right as another footpath joins, to reach the road again, and then turn left **Ⓒ**.

At the corner by Pont Poultry Farm turn right off the road up a pleasant grassy track. This becomes quite a climb until a white gate appears ahead. Pass through this to reach the church of Lanteglos-by-Fowey **Ⓓ**.

The lovely church stands in this seemingly lonely position because it was built to serve Polruan and the four scattered hamlets of the peninsula: thus it is more or less central for all the district. It is dedicated to St Wyllow, a Christian hermit living in this part of Cornwall long before St Augustine and his followers landed in Kent in 597. He is believed to have been killed close to the head of the creek, a martyr to his faith. A few fragments of a Norman church survive in the existing fabric, though most of what we see today dates from the 14th century. The church was fortunate in not being over-restored in the 19th century, although drastic repairs had to be made between 1896 and 1906.

From the porch leave the churchyard by the eastern gate, turning left down the lane. This soon climbs quite steeply to pass the National Trust's Pencarrow car park on the left before reaching the main road. Turn right here, and then after 200 yds (184m) left over a stile, crossing a field towards Pencarrow Head. Keep the hedge on your left.

At the next stile **E** there is a choice: keep straight on if you wish to explore the headland and enjoy its views, or

Fowey from Polruan

turn to the right (with or without crossing the stile) to take the coastal path back to Polruan. This has very steep ups and downs but is enjoyable, both for the exercise it demands and for the scenery. The two Lantic beaches can be seen below and are accessible by a very steep path.

From Blackbottle Rock, another excellent viewpoint, the village is visible ahead, though this is deceptive as a fair walk is involved before you get there. After a stile by a stream fork left to keep on the coastal path. Polruan's top car park is reached by passing through a gate to the right of a white house. Turn left on to the road to find the car park by a school with a belfry. If you are parked on the quay descend to it by Tinker's Hill. ●

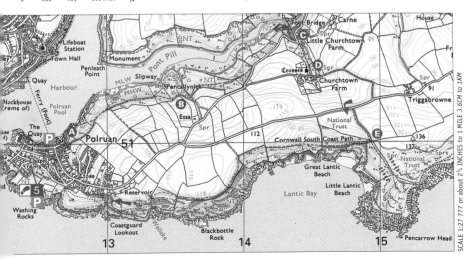

Prussia Cove and Cudden Point

Start	Perranuthnoe, just south of the A394, between Helston and Penzance
Distance	4½ miles (7.25km)
Approximate time	3 hours
Parking	Beach car park, opposite Perranuthnoe post office
Refreshments	Pub at Perranuthnoe
Ordnance Survey maps	Landranger 203 (Land's End) and Explorer 7 (Land's End)

The outward part of the walk is through fertile agricultural land – cabbage-growing country – using field paths and ancient tracks. The return leg is along one of the most interesting parts of the Coastal Path, taking in romantic Prussia Cove and superb views of Mount's Bay after Cudden Point.

Leave the car park at the seaward end and turn immediately left along a made-up lane which is the coastal footpath. When this divides, take the left fork uphill (keeping to the made-up lane). This threads its way between modern bungalows to reach a rather overgrown green path at the top, passing a bungalow called Lismore on the right. Climb over a stile into a meadow and climb to the farm (Trebarvah) at the top, crossing another stile into the farmyard.

The path continues eastwards across the road that leads into the farmyard from the north. It leads to the left of the topmost cowshed, beginning as a muddy cow-track which immediately leads into a meadow (reached by a stone stile). Keep the hedge on your left for about 100 yds (92m) and cross the stile on the left **Ⓐ**. Skirt the field, with the hedge to the right, and go over the next stile, keeping the hedge on the right. After the next stile keep straight on to the far hedge and turn right, now keeping the hedge on the left. The next stile leads into a.farm lane, then almost immediately go over the stile on the right and walk parallel with the lane inside the field. The path comes out on the lane again for a short distance before reaching the road.

Turn left and walk along the road for 50 yds (46m). Turn right over a stile and walk along the edge of a market garden with the hedge on your right. At

Prussia Cove

the far end of the market garden cross over the stile on the right and continue in the field, with the hedge to the left. This soon leads into a grassy lane: go through an iron gate on to the road. Turn left up the hill to pass a line of bungalows on the right. After these, take the track on the right **B** which leads round the southern edge of Rosudgeon Common. This is rather scruffy. At the end turn right on to a footpath. Bear right where this path divides **C** to join a farm track which soon meets with the lane entering Higher Kenneggy. Turn right past the farmhouse and campsite.

After a while the lane becomes a pleasant and ancient enclosed path which looks as though it could once have been used by the notorious smugglers of the district. Eventually it emerges on to Kenneggy Cliff **D** where one path plunges down to the beach, but ours descends more gently to the right to meet with the South Coast Path (bear right on reaching this). There is a good view from here of the wicked rocks known as The Enys which shelter Bessy's Cove, popularly known as Prussia Cove **E**. Apparently as a boy the notorious smuggler John Carter enjoyed playing the game known as King of Prussia, which is how his hideout came by this name.

The curious granite-built house (Porth-enalls) is either romantic or sinister according to taste. The coastal footpath passes by its entrance and follows its drive, leaving it at the gate to head towards the picturesque cove-side cottages, one of which is thatched. It then reaches some even more photogenic fishermen's retreats; again one is thatched, and another has a roof of corrugated steel which is held down with chains. The path follows every nuance of this tortuous shoreline, up hills and down dales, but every step is another scenic delight.

The National Trust owns the magnificent headland of Cudden Point and from here the view across Mount's Bay opens up. St Michael's Mount holds centre stage with Penzance just to the left. Perranuthnoe is in the right foreground, its church tower prominent. It is important to look back as well – the Lizard is well seen from here. Animals have the wit to lie low until walkers have passed; I looked back a little later and saw an agile fox climbing the cliffs below Acton Castle.

Approaching Perranuthnoe the path passes by a line of declining tamarisks. Through the next field head for the bottom left-hand corner to the lowest path which follows on the seaward side of a line of concrete fence-posts. The coastal path is now clearly waymarked back to the starting point at the car park at Perranuthnoe. ●

Porthcurno, Porthgwarra and St Levan's Church

Start	Porthcurno
Distance	4 miles (6.5km)
Approximate time	2½ hours
Parking	Porthcurno beach car park
Refreshments	Cafés at Porthcurno and Porthgwarra
Ordnance Survey maps	Landranger 203 (Land's End) and Explorer 7 (Land's End)

In this area of west Cornwall the maps are sometimes rather optimistic about rights of way inland from the coastal path, and here the section of the route beyond Ardensawah Cliff has become neglected. Those wearing shorts may have an uncomfortable time negotiating the narrow path through gorse, but it is well worth the short-lived discomfort.

The starting point in the beach car park at Porthcurno may seem pointless to those who know that they can leave their cars for nothing in the Minack Theatre car park at the top of the cliff. Doing this, however, makes a short walk even shorter and misses a lovely though energetic beginning.

Leave the lower car park and take the path to the beach. Bear to the right almost immediately on the footpath signposted to Minack. An alternative route is soon offered on the right, which may be more suitable for the young or elderly. Nonetheless the way to the left, threading through the cliffs which provide such a romantic backdrop for the theatre, is not excessively difficult. The steep climb ends at the theatre's car park: cross this to find a path on the far side. This leads to the spectacular headland of Pedn-mên-an-mere **Ⓐ**, though the National Trust prefers to call this property

Rospletha Cliffs. The gradual descent to Porth Chapel is in contrast to the steep climb up on the other side of the cove. The tower of St Levan's Church can be clearly seen to landward.

After the ascent from Porth Chapel the coastal path reaches Carn Barges, with more dramatic scenery, before descending to Porthgwarra **Ⓑ**. Note the perched rock on the left and the landmarks on the hill ahead.

As you climb the coastal path from Porthgwarra you will probably hear the eery sound of the Runnel Stone Buoy, a mile or so out to sea. After Hella Point the jagged rocks around Polostoc Zawn and Gwennap Head remind us how perilous this coastline was in the days of sail. Land's End can now be clearly seen in the distance. The reddish colour of the intricately-jointed rocks of the cliffs contrasts with the green hue of those at the top covered with lichen. A maze of footpaths wanders across Carn

Guthensbrâs: try to stay with the one that follows the coastline. After the carn there is a steep ascent and the path passes through a stone wall, heading for the tower of Sennen church. On the left is a rock on which nature has carved an impression of an eagle's head.

Turn right at a footpath crossroads to follow a faint path towards a grey house on the skyline; there is a ruined cottage to the left. The path now threads a faint way through painful gorse to meet **C** a track coming from Ardensawah: this is a bridleway. Pass through an old iron gate to approach the grey house. Turn left on to a concrete driveway to meet the lane going to Porthgwarra, then turn right. About 200 yds (184m) down the lane notice a disused footpath which once went to Raftra – the formerly wide path is now completely choked with undergrowth and utterly impassable.

Fortunately our route takes the next footpath on the left which is to be found soon after the lane narrows and the word 'SLOW' is painted on its surface. Here **D** there is a stile on the left, and from it you will see the tower of St Levan's Church. Follow the path down with the hedge on the right. Cross the stile ahead to continue on the same course but now with the hedge on the left. The fields here are very small, sometimes only three or four acres.

Carry straight on over another stile (these were designed to be crossed without losing one's stride). A series of stiles follows along the path to the cottages by St Levan's Church. This has the dignified simplicity characteristic of medieval Cornish churches; in the churchyard is the split rock which is said to have been St Levan's favourite place of repose. He prophesied that if a donkey should ever be driven through the cleft the world would end.

Leave the churchyard over the stile by the ancient cross on its eastern side (behind the church). Cross the stile at the top of the field and follow the path over the next field past the remains of another ancient cross. The path leads into Rospletha farmyard and emerges on to the lane which leads down to the starting point, passing close to the theatre car park *en route*. ●

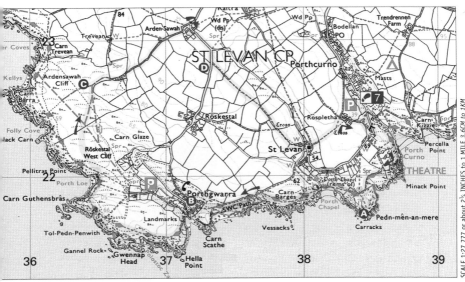

Efford Down and the Bude Canal

Start	Bude tourist information centre, Crescent car park
Distance	5 miles (8km)
Approximate time	3 hours
Parking	Crescent car park at Bude
Refreshments	Cafés and pubs at Bude, pub at Marhamchurch
Ordnance Survey maps	Landranger 190 (Bude & Clovelly) and Pathfinder 1292, SS 20/30 (Bude & Holsworthy)

After the initial steepish climb up to Compass Point there is nothing too intimidating. The path follows quite close to the road after Upton, but it is far enough away for well-behaved dogs to run free. When the path leaves the coastline it follows a pleasant route over the fields to reach the canal at Helebridge. The canalside walk back to Bude is quiet and peaceful.

Leave the car park and cross the bridge by the Falcon Hotel. Turn to the right to pass the church, graveyard, and some modern houses. Look for a stile on the left leading on to the down. Follow the path up towards Compass Point with the watch-tower on the right. The summit is a wonderful viewpoint, though the town is not very beautiful to the east. The coastal path continues to climb to reach Efford Beacon **A** where there is a topograph showing the various headlands and moorland summits visible on a clear day. It does not mark the outstanding landmark – the radar dishes at Coombe. On a good day Lundy Island may be seen to the north, Trevose Head to the south.

The path descends gently to Upton where it runs parallel to the road, but far enough away from it to allow dogs to run free. The path continues by the road past the headlands of Higher and Lower Longbeak. Take the path to the

left at the Salthouse **B**, which as the name suggests was an old salt store in the 18th century but is now a holiday home. Cross the road and take the footpath signposted to Helebridge by the Marine Drive signboard.

Cross the meadow to its top left-hand corner and use the stile into the next field which is crossed diagonally by a well-trodden path. Climb another stile and follow the wall on the right which is made of rounded stones, obviously

Bude from Efford Down

taken from the beach. The whitewashed cottages of Marhamchurch can be seen ahead. Beyond the next stile the path descends the field diagonally, heading for the bridge on the main road below. Turn right on to a concrete road and then left on to the main road **C**.

Cross the bridge to visit the building on the wharf which houses fascinating relics of the Bude Canal and explains its operation (further, more detailed, explanation can be found at the Folk Museum by the sea lockgates at Bude). The unique feature of the canal was the way gradients were overcome. Barges, hauled by horses towing four or five at a time, had wheels and were pulled up inclines by a novel use of water power. Enormous tubs of water, used as weights, were lowered into 220-ft (67m) pits, and chains were fixed to the barges to haul them up the slopes. When the chains broke, the effect was cataclysmic: the tub, containing tons of water, crashed to the bottom of the pit, letting the barge run out of control to the base of the slope. Its crew had to leap for their lives. The canal carried fertiliser and sea sand to small towns in the interior of Cornwall. It became uneconomic in the 1880s and was abandoned.

Re-cross the bridge to the tow-path which follows the left bank of the canal. Although the walking is now

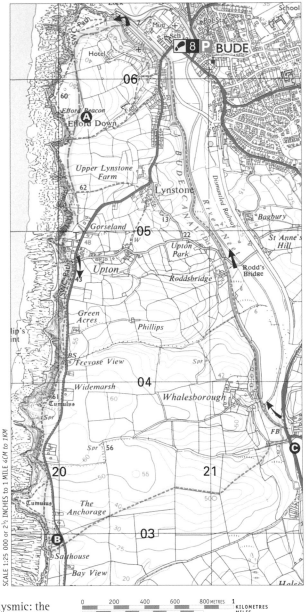

level it remains enjoyable. The coarse fishing here is rewarding. At Rodd's Bridge the path crosses to the other side of the canal. The old locks of this revived section of the canal have been converted into weirs. Just before Bude the canal is part of a nature reserve. Before the path reaches the road again, turn to the right into the car park. ●

St Anthony Head and St Mawes Harbour

Start	Porth Farm, between Portscatho and St Anthony
Distance	6 miles (9.5km)
Approximate time	3 hours
Parking	Porth Farm car park (National Trust)
Refreshments	None
Ordnance Survey maps	Landranger 204 (Truro & Falmouth) and Pathfinder 1366, SW 83/73/93 (Falmouth & St Mawes)

This route follows a pattern that seems almost standard for a number of these walks – a bracing section of cliff-walking followed by a more sheltered passage by a tree-fringed creek. Here, however, there is an enjoyable in-between part alongside the mouth of a wide estuary which gives unique views of St Mawes and its river.

Cross the road and pass the toilets to take the path to the beach, but bear to the right rather than descending to Towan Beach. The South Coast Path follows along the edge of a low cliff, from where there is a good view back across Veryan Bay. A little further on, from Killigerran Head **Ⓐ**, there is an even better view ahead, across Porthbeor Beach to Carrick Roads, with the Lizard beyond, the telecommunication dishes on Goonhilly being clearly visible.

A long steady climb follows, and suddenly the town of Falmouth is revealed on the right as the path rounds Zone Point. Only the lantern of St Anthony's lighthouse can be seen from this side of the promontory. On the headland itself **Ⓑ**, which has many visitors due to the convenient car park, the remains of an old gun battery, operational right up until 1956, now serve a new purpose as toilets and National Trust Information Centre.

Walk through the car park and near its entrance take the path leading down to Molunan Beach; or alternatively you can take the coast path to the lighthouse and reach the beach that way. The path down is steep, and of course there will be an equally steep climb on the other side. A lovely group of Scots pines on the far side of Molunan provides a perfect frame for the view of Falmouth across the estuary. Sheep graze on the edges of precipitous rocks above the water.

St Mawes is well seen from here. A whole flock of oystercatchers perch precariously on one half-submerged rock: why do they choose to congregate on this one rock when so many more are available?

Before Amsterdam Point **Ⓒ** head for the top of the copse, where there is a convenient seat ideal for watching the shipping. Go down the hill to Cellars Beach and the road which passes behind Place House. The church adjoining the mansion is a sad building. A notice seeks a benefactor for it, saying that the Spry-Grant Dalton family is no longer responsible for its upkeep. There is a lovely Spry monument in the north chancel. The sanctuary is suffering badly from damp – how long will it stand?

Turn left after leaving the churchyard towards Place Quay. There are wonderful lilies outside the walled gardens of Place House. At the quay follow the path with the creek on the left. Pass through a gate into Drawler Plantation. This is a very twisty, up-and-down path. The signpost says that it is only 1¼ miles (2km) back to Porth Farm, but it takes nearly an hour to return, perhaps due to the numerous seats *en route*, all of which are

Place House

conveniently sited at viewpoints.

The path bends first at the entrance to Porth Creek (North-hill Point) **D**, and then at the ivy-clad house of Froe, where the road can be seen on the other side of the creek. A long footbridge takes the path across the muddy head of the pill. Turn right on to a path which runs parallel to the road to the lower car park in front of Porth Farm. ●

```
0      200    400    600   800 METRES   1
                                         KILOMETRES
                                         MILES
0      200    400    600 YARDS    ½
```

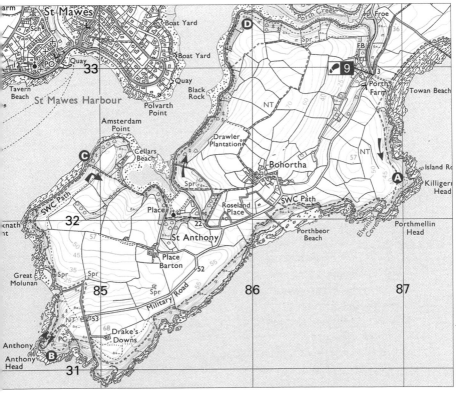

Stepper Point from Trevone

Start	Trevone Bay, west of Padstow
Distance	7 miles (11.25km)
Approximate time	3 hours
Parking	Car parks at Trevone Bay
Refreshments	Seasonal cafés at Trevone Bay
Ordnance Survey maps	Landranger 200 (Newquay) and Pathfinder 1337, SW 87/97 (Padstow & Wadebridge)

This pleasant, fairly energetic walk covers a variety of coastal scenery with a contrasting inland section crossing the peninsula. The cliffs are exposed and lofty – be very careful if it is windy.

The car parks are on the north-eastern side of Trevone Bay. Take the coastal path which climbs to the clifftop, with the remarkable Round Hole **A** on the right. If the weather is rough flecks of foam at the bottom show that there is a passage to the sea. It is a fascinating and rare landform, illustrating how the sea exploits weaknesses in geological strata. There are excellent views westwards from Roundhole Point and further on at Porthmissen there is another phenomenon – a rock bridge.

Note the contortions of the strata in the cliffs here; there are good views westwards to Trevose Head. The walking is delightful with springy turf underfoot. Ahead is a spectacular rock pinnacle; note too the fine view back. A steep climb leads to the cliffs above the pinnacle. Gulland Rock is offshore to the left, and as the path nears Gunver Head another deadly group of rocks known as King Phillip appears ahead off Pentire Head. The tower on Stepper Point comes into view.

At the Butter Hole the slaty rock is a wonderful deep blue to purple, with a sandy beach far below. The awful inevitability of shipwreck for a sailing-ship embayed by an onshore wind must have inspired many a prayer here.

The Pepperpot on Stepper Point **B**, also known as the Daymark, is fenced-off and dangerous to explore. The coastal footpath goes down here, though most people will prefer the upper path which will not involve so much climbing and passes in front of the abandoned coastguard lookout.

The path now follows the shore of the estuary, where the tide flows very fast and the Doom Bar was aptly named; certainly the sound of the surf here can be quite frightening.

At Hawker's Cove there is a deserted lifeboat station. The road ends here. It is possible to cut a corner by crossing the sands where the path suddenly turns west to skirt an inlet, but be warned that the tide comes in quickly. After the inlet the view of the River Camel ahead is stunning – the Rock ferry can be seen in the distance. If the tide is out the walk along the beach, rather than on the low cliffs, is a pleasant change. St George's Cove is an inviting place for a picnic or a paddle, though dogs are forbidden.

Our path turns off to the right before

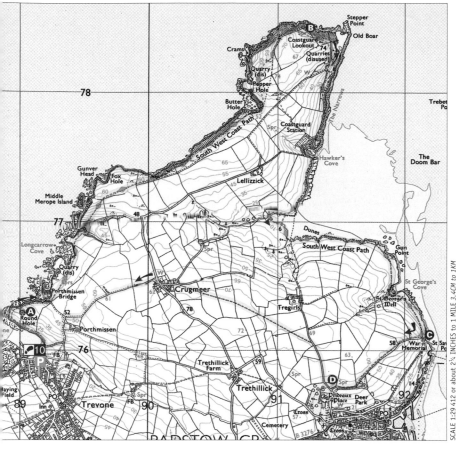

SCALE 1:29.412 or about 2¼ INCHES to 1 MILE 3.4CM to 1KM

0	200	400	600	800 METRES	1
					KILOMETRES
					MILES
0	200	400	600 YARDS	½	

the railings of the War Memorial **C**, but it would be a shame not to take the few extra steps as the view is memorable. Should you wish to visit Padstow keep on the coastal path and then rejoin this route via the lane past Prideaux Place.

Climb up on the edge of the fields with the hedge on the left. This is a pleasant field walk, giving occasional glimpses of Padstow and its river. It soon reaches the perimeter wall of the Prideaux Place Deer Park. Turn right on to the lane **D** and where this becomes level, after about 500 yds (455m), there is a footpath sign and steps on the left. Climb these and cross the field diagonally (if the field is cropped, turn

left a little further on to follow a farm track down the far side of the field). There is a stone stile before the gate which leads into another field which is also crossed diagonally. Cross straight over the next small field and the following one diagonally, noticing the lovely view. Head for the buildings over the next field. There are now just two more fields to cross before reaching a track which leads to the small settlement of Crugmeer.

Turn to the right along the road for a very short distance before taking a farm track on the left leading towards some old huts. Pass through the gate by these and continue along the track which zigzags before passing in front of Porthmissen Farm. It then drops steeply to reach the car parks at Trevone Bay. ●

Falmouth Bay and the Helford River

Falmouth Bay and the Helford River

Start	Maenporth Beach, south of Falmouth
Distance	5 miles (8km)
Approximate time	2½ hours
Parking	Free parking on beach, other (paying) car parks behind
Refreshments	Beach cafés and pub at Maenporth, pub at Mawnan Smith
Ordnance Survey maps	Landranger 204 (Truro & Falmouth) and Explorer 8 (The Lizard)

The least interesting part of this walk is the beginning: the path follows the cliff's edge, but is squeezed in behind undergrowth which hides the view and the back gardens of the properties overlooking the shore. After about ten minutes, however, things improve, and the section to Rosemullion Head shows Cornish coastal scenery at its most memorable. A pleasant path through clifftop woodland follows, leading to Toll Point, a magnificent viewpoint for the Helford River. The return alternates woodland walking with field paths. There are few difficult gradients.

The footpath begins on the southern edge of Maenporth Beach. Keep to the right of the wire fence at the top of the low cliffs. A short enclosed stretch follows with garden fences on one side and a dense hedge on the other, seaward, side which screens the view of the sea. The path soon emerges, however, to give a fine view of the way ahead to the south; the Hutches are the line of rocks below. Cross a stile to follow the edge of a field. The path descends to sea level at Bream Cove below the Meudon Vean Hotel. It then enters the National Trust property of Nansidwell and soon descends to another beach (Gatamala Cove) before climbing back up again to reach Rosemullion Head **Ⓐ**

This wonderful viewpoint also belongs to the National Trust. On a clear day there are views across Falmouth Bay to the Roseland peninsula and beyond, while in the opposite direction the dangerous coastline of the Lizard can be seen.

After the headland keep on the seaward side of a meadow to a stile on the far side. At Mawnan Glebe (National Trust) the path threads its way through shady woodland (a welcome relief this, on a hot summer's day). At Shag Rock the trees end to give a view along the rocky Parson's Beach. Broad, grassy downland follows, giving superb panoramas of the Helford River. The headland of Toll Point provides the best viewpoint.

The path now descends to the river at Porthallack, climbing again behind the old boathouse to reach the little beach of Porth Saxon with its slipway. Turn to the right here **B** up the beautiful Carwinion Valley (National Trust). This is a delightful woodland path following the course of a stream which has its source in Mawnan Smith village. At the house at the top of the path continue up past modern homes on the left to reach a road by the Mawnan Smith village sign.

Turn left here towards the village and after about 200 yds (184m) and some more modern housing look for a well-concealed footpath to Meudon on the right **C**. (Should you want refreshment at this point continue on the road into Mawnan Smith.)

The path through the meadows overlooks the village on the left. Pass through the gate at the top through another field, keeping the hedge on the right. The weird cries are from the peacocks at the Meudon Vean Hotel. At the top make for the gateway into the farmyard at the top, but do not go through it. Instead turn left along the hedge, following a footpath sign to Carlidnack, and cross the stile into a narrow downhill meadow. Where this becomes an enclosed lane look for a small gateway on the right. Pass through this and go down steep steps into a meadow. Cross this diagonally looking for an opening to the left. Continue downhill through the next meadow

heading just to the right of the house with the red roof.

Do not cross the stream **D** but turn right to follow it. Note the superb ash trees before a stile on the left leads into woods. You may take either of the paths where the main path divides. Excavations suggest that there may be badgers in this wood. The paths rejoin and leave the wood by a stile into a meadow: the great joy of this walk lies in the way that the path alternates between woodland and open countryside. Finally the path descends to Maenporth through meadows. Keep the fence to the left and reach the southern end of the beach conveniently close to a café and a pub. ●

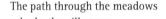

Helford, Little Dennis and Manaccan

Start	Helford
Distance	5 miles (8km)
Approximate time	2½ hours
Parking	Helford car park
Refreshments	Pub and tea-garden at Helford, pub at Manaccan
Ordnance Survey maps	Landranger 204 (Truro & Falmouth) and Explorer 8 (The Lizard)

This is a route which shows all the features typical of the countryside of south Cornwall: the ria (the lower reaches of a river valley invaded by the sea), a fine headland affording grand views of the coastline, an estuary which is a sanctuary for waders and much other birdlife, ancient woodland, a charming village, and a walk over the fields. How could that be improved?
Note the one drawback to this walk – the Bosahan Estate forbids dogs on the concessionary footpath which follows the Helford River through its land.

Turn left out of the car park towards the sailing club, but before reaching it look for a kissing-gate on the right which leads into woods. Go down steps to a road, turn right and climb up to find a notice on the left at a bend. The notice concerns the concessionary footpath to St Anthony, and expressly forbids dogs. If you are indeed dogless turn up here, having taken in the lovely views of the river. Ironically you pass the disued dog-kennels of the Bosahan Estate on the right. The tame pheasants here testify to the reason for the ban on dogs. The path

drops to the first of the lovely riverside beaches – Bosahan Cove – which has smooth sand and clear water.

The narrow path continues to twist through trees before it reaches another

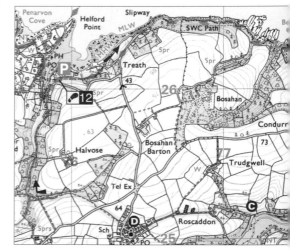

lovely beach – Ponsence Cove  –
where it is hard to resist a paddle. The
luxuriant growth of the trees hides the
river for much of the way, even after
The Gew where the path turns to the
south-east.

Pass through a kissing-gate and over
a stile to reach the Little Dennis
peninsula. There are wide views to the
north with the St Anthony lighthouse
an easily recognisable landmark. The
other St Anthony (-in-Meneage) is
much closer, and is soon visible to the
right as the path reaches a meadow
which is level with the top of its church
tower. Climb up on the seaward edge of
a field to a track going through banks
of gorse. On the left there is a country
footpath sign and a stile. Follow the
circular path which has been cleared
through the gorse to reach Dennis Head
B. This gives an even better view of
Falmouth Bay to the north, while Gillan
is the village across the inlet in the
other direction. Nare Point is the
headland. Return to the stile and turn
right on to the track. When it emerges
from the gorse, cross the field ahead,
making for a cream-coloured house.

Helford River

Follow the track here down to a gate
and go through this to reach
St Anthony's Church, a famous beauty
spot surrounded by pines, palms and
fuchsias. It is often locked, however,
because of vandalism and theft.

Now follow the lane alongside the
river. The salt-flats and the woods
which form the backdrop support a
variety of bird-life: herons, curlews,
oystercatchers etc. The heron's harsh
call contrasts with the sweetness of the
songs of the blackbird and thrush.

Where the road descends to the creek
again look for a path to Manaccan on
the right **C**. This goes up though the
woods along a very ancient sunken
way. When it reaches Roscaddon it
continues on concrete to Manaccan
church **D**, which may also be locked.
Go through the churchyard (there is a
shop along the lane on the left while
the pub is at the lower, southern, end of
the village) and turn sharp right up the
hill to pass the school. Opposite the
garage turn left on to the footpath to
Helford, crossing the field with the
hedge on the right. Cross the road and
descend to a wood. Turn left, follow the
path across the corner of a field to a
stile at the bottom. The path now
follows a lovely little wooded valley,
finally reaching Helford village. Keep
the river on the left to the car park or
turn left to find the Shipwright's Arms
and the tea-garden. ●

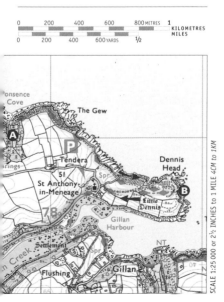

SCALE 1:25 000 or 2½ INCHES to 1 MILE 4CM to 1KM

Hawker Country – Morwenstow & Marsland Mouth

Hawker Country – Morwenstow and Marsland Mouth

Start	Morwenstow, north of Bude
Distance	4½ miles (7.25km)
Approximate time	3 hours
Parking	At Morwenstow Church
Refreshments	Rectory Tea Room at car park; the Bush Inn at Crosstown, ¼ mile (400m) east of the church
Ordnance Survey maps	Landranger 190 (Bude) and Pathfinder 1273, SS 21/31 (Kilkhampton)

On the map this looks a short walk so that the time taken seems surprising. Perhaps it is explained by the fascinating church at the start, and by the lonely, savage beauty of Marsland Mouth, where Cornwall meets Devon and it is hard not to linger. There is strenuous climbing on this route.

There can be few churches that have a more dramatic location than the one at Morwenstow. Situated on the edge of a small valley that tumbles to the sea within ½ mile (800m), it is inevitable that the church should have strong maritime connections. Many a dead sailor lies buried in the churchyard – the famous white figurehead (removed for repair in 1989) came from the *Caledonia*, a Scottish brig which was wrecked off Morwenstow in 1842. Only one of her crew of ten seamen survived, the captain being buried beneath the site of the figurehead (on the left of the church path, just below the lych-gate), while the rest of the crew, along with many other victims of the sea, are buried by the 'Upper Trees' where a tall granite cross bearing the words 'Unknown yet Well Known' marks the site of the communal grave.

This information comes from the peerless guide to the church which is crammed full of facts about the lovely building and its famous vicar from 1834, Robert Stephen Hawker. He is credited with being the inventor of the harvest festival – the first one took place at Morwenstow in 1843, a celebration for good crops after years of famine – though he is better known for his literary work and philanthropy.

Our walk starts at the lych-gate: head straight down through the churchyard to a stone stile next to Hawker's vicarage, now a private house. The curious chimneys of the building are said to represent the towers of various churches with which Hawker was associated, and that of his Oxford college. The path descends through trees to a footbridge at the bottom of the valley, and then climbs the other

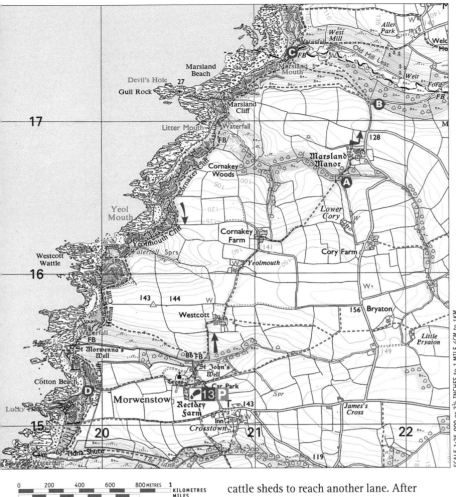

SCALE 1:25 000 or 2½ INCHES to 1 MILE 4CM to 1KM

0	200	400	600	800 METRES	1

KILOMETRES
MILES

0	200	400	600 YARDS	½

side equally steeply. Keep straight on at a footpath junction to reach the top. Pass through a gate and continue with the hedge on the right. After 50 yds (46m) turn right through another gate into a very muddy farmyard. Having struggled through this turn to the left up a concrete road.

Leave this by keeping straight on where the road bends to the right. Keep the hedge on the left and eventually cross a stile at Yeolmouth, turning right into a lane. Bear left when this meets with a made-up road, descending to a farmyard and turning right past the cattle sheds to reach another lane. After a muddy patch this improves to provide good walking with fine views ahead. Turn to the left after the gate at the end of the track and keep the hedge on the left to reach a stile at the bottom right-hand corner of the field (it may be possible to cross it diagonally).

Bear slightly left to the woods at the bottom of the next field, heading for the buildings beyond the trees. Cross a stile and climb down a very steep bank, made easy by rough-cut steps, to a smart new footbridge **A** at the bottom. On the opposite side of the valley the path uses part of an ancient track made gloomy by its steep banks. Bear right at the footpath junction at the top and climb up to the buildings ahead. The footpath passes through the farmyard of Marsland Manor to reach the lane where you turn left.

At the junction take the 'Unsuitable for Motors' lane signposted to Marsland Mouth. Pass through the gate and bear to the left when the paths divide **Ⓑ**. It is very worthwhile to make a descent to sea level rather than taking other paths offered on the left which stay high on the side or top of the valley. This is especially the case if there is a good sea running (and there usually is, here). The Mouth is a wonderful wild place, often utterly deserted – the loneliness is exhilarating. If you cross the stream **Ⓒ** you are in Devon, and you have to do this to reach the beach – an excellent place to picnic.

Climb back from the beach, cross the bridge back into Cornwall, and take the coast path on the right. Of course it is a steep climb, but the views back are rewarding. Note the contorted strata of Gull Rock below and the fine view inland. There is a seat at the top so you can regain breath and enjoy the view before the descent to Litter Mouth, which is helped by good steps; there are none for the climb on the other side, which is a hard 15-minute slog.

The procedure is repeated at Yeol Mouth. Then there is a short stretch of level ground along Henna Cliff before the descent to Morwenstow begins. The sinister radar dishes at Coombe are now in view ahead. The final up-and-down comes at Morwenstow itself, the climb up to Vicarage (or Rectory) Cliff **Ⓓ** being made for the superb view to the south-west, the inspiration for many of Hawker's verses. This is coastal scenery at its most awesome. Turn to the left at the gate at the top of the cliff to return to Morwenstow church.　●

Morwenstow church

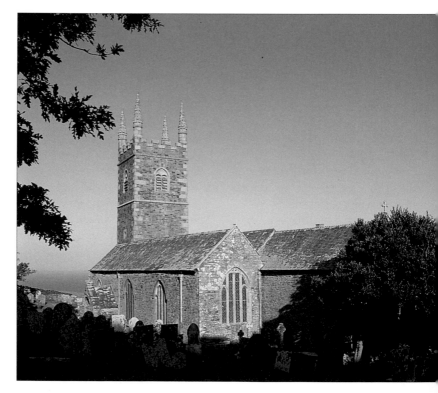

Land's End and Nanjizal from Sennen

Start	Sennen harbour
Distance	5½ miles (8.75km)
Approximate time	3 hours
Parking	Car park at Sennen harbour
Refreshments	Pubs at Sennen and Land's End
Ordnance Survey maps	Landranger 203 (Land's End) and Explorer 7 (Land's End)

The romance of Land's End has all but vanished under commercial pressures, but these only extend for about ½ mile (800m) from the car park. This walk offers the opportunity of enjoying the grandeur that survives. With the sun setting in the western sea, this walk will live in the memory forever.

From Sennen harbour make for the castellated lookout **A** on the clifftop to the south-west; the footpath is signposted to Mayon Cliff, which extends from Sennen to Land's End. Follow the coast path up concrete steps: from the watch-tower there are fine views of Land's End and the Longships. Continue along the (badly-eroded) path around the top of the cliffs. This is one of the most frequented footpaths in England, but also one of the best scenically. Note the statuesque Irish Lady below – a detached block of rock perched precariously on top of a pinnacle. Another weirdly eroded rock that is passed is known as Dr Syntax's Head. Bear to the right if you wish to look at the gifts in the First and Last House, but take the left fork to reach the Hotel **B** and its attractions more directly. This is the free way to visit the place, but you will not be able to see 'The Land's End Experience' without paying.

Land's End provides excellent free playground facilities for children, and parents can watch from the terrace of the Longships Bar.

Next make for the white Greeb Cottage to the south, which is the headquarters of a small wildlife park. There is also a model village here. Pass behind the animal enclosures to a signpost. Now the way is more like a proper coastal footpath. The sunset picture that is a classic for landscape photographers is taken from near Carn Cheer **C** and includes the rock stacks known as Enys Dodnan and the Armed Knight with the Longships lighthouse in the background.

The next ½ mile (800m) or so must rank with the best of any of Cornwall's coastal walking. The granite is of a unique pink hue near the sea, but lichen makes it green elsewhere. The white house ahead overlooks Nanjizal. Note the amazing Cornish 'hedges' here, enclosing impossibly tiny fields.

SCALE 1:27 777 or about 2½ INCHES to 1 MILE 3.6CM to 1KM

0	200	400	600	800 METRES	1
					KILOMETRES
					MILES
0	200	400	600 YARDS	½	

The path is narrow, often occupying a ledge on precipitous cliffs. Words cannot do justice to the grandeur of this scenery.

Do not descend to the beach at Nanjizal but look for a faint path **D** that climbs through the gorse on the side of the valley to the top opposite the white house. Follow the path along the top of the valley for about ½ mile (800m), keeping the wall on your left. At the end of the path **E**, there is a stone stile on the left. Climb over this and cross the field to its left-hand corner, making for the tower of Sennen church (if dusk is falling do not worry unduly: the evening light lingers for ages here in the summer).

Cut the corner of the next field, making for the top of the left hedge (the church should be in view again here). Keep the hedge on the left to the farm.

Keep straight on past the first of three farmyards, crossing a stone stile to pass through the last one to reach stone steps by a gate on the far side (the farmhouse is on the left). Follow the right edge of a field past an ancient cross. After steps and a gate at the end of the field head for a cottage ahead, and pass through its garden to reach the road. Go straight on to join the main road close to the Wreckers pub. Turn right, and pass the First and Last pub and Sennen church. Opposite the supermarket, but before the petrol station, turn left down a footpath **F** which descends directly to Sennen harbour, the starting point. ●

Mount Edgcumbe, the Sound and Cawsand

Start	Cremyll, on the west side of the Tamar
Distance	6 miles (9.5km)
Approximate time	3 hours
Parking	Mount Edgcumbe Country Park car park, Cremyll
Refreshments	Pubs at Cremyll and Cawsand, tearooms at Maker and Cawsand
Ordnance Survey maps	Landranger 201 (Plymouth & Launceston) and Pathfinder 1356, SX 45/55 (Plymouth)

Although at an early point a notice warns of 'Dangerous cliffs and paths', there is really nothing to fear. The paths through the country park can be steep at times, it is true, but are not dangerous. Woodland alternates with wide coastal vistas, those of Plymouth and its Sound being particularly memorable. The village of Cawsand, a mini-resort, is an excellent halfway point, and the return leg is pastoral, passing by the lovely church at Maker to the northern side of the peninsula, and continuing to Cremyll by the shore of the Tamar River.

The Cremyll ferry was once an important gateway into Cornwall, the road continuing to Looe and Lostwithiel. At Cremyll make for the entrance to Mount Edgcumbe, where the coastal footpath sign points the way into the country park. This is the route that we follow, as it skirts the formal gardens on the southern, seaward, side of the park. The house, which is seen well from the gates, is still the seat of the Earls of Mount Edgcumbe even though the original mansion was destroyed by German incendiary bombs in 1941. The house was rebuilt, maintaining the tradition of residence by the family which dates from the time of Henry VIII.

The coastal path follows the shoreline along a concrete road, passing a pond **A** and a classical temple. The views of Plymouth and its Sound are magnificent. Soon after the point where the concrete road lapses into a well-used path, there is a sign warning of dangerous cliffs and paths. Beyond this the path climbs to a gate, with a romantic ruined lookout tower – which is in fact a folly – on the right.

The path soon divides, but it hardly matters which fork one takes. The upper path leads to the half-timbered Lady Emma's Cottage from which there is a splendid view framed by pine trees. A zigzag path now leads to an upper path and another folly – a ruined arch. An old breakwater can be seen through the trees far below: this is Picklecombe Point. On the right there is a shady grotto to rest in.

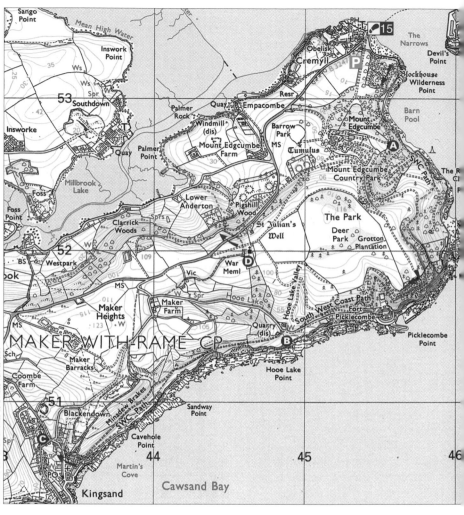

After Picklecombe bear left to the road below following the coastal footpath signs. Cawsand can now be seen ahead. Leave the country park by a gate and then cross a stile. Turn right into the lane, then almost immediately left off it **B**. A pleasant stretch follows over grassy downland into the twin villages of Kingsand and Cawsand, rivals still and once renowned for their smuggling activities.

The path emerges conveniently close to a pub, though our route turns sharp right into Lower Row which leads to the road to Millbrook. Just before the main road look for a steep lane on the right **C**, the Earl's Drive. Take this and climb to pass behind the fort. The going is less strenuous now, and although a field path is offered on the left (signposted to Maker church) it is easier to keep to the lane, turning right to pass the main gate of Maker Farm on the right.

Now look for a footpath on the left leading to Maker church. This brings a surprise in the form of the tea-garden at Friary Manor – on a hot day this could be taken as a mirage! Cross the drive to follow the path to a meadow. Keep the hedge on the left and then cross over a stile so that the hedge is on the right. From the next stile there is an extensive view to Torpoint, Millbrook Lake, and Plymouth.

Maker church **D** is well worth a visit. The name is derived from a Cornish word meaning 'ruin'. Although it was restored quite comprehensively in the 19th century, it retains the characteristic grace and charm of the traditional Cornish church and dates from the 15th century. Just to the north of the church, and hidden in the woods, is St Julian's Well, an ancient oratory dedicated to the 5th-century Cornish saint who is the patron saint of ferrymen. Art lovers will enjoy the copy of the portrait of Thomas Smart which hangs in the church. He was vicar here from 1717 until 1735 and was the first subject to be painted by Sir Joshua Reynolds. Aged 12, the young artist sketched the vicar from the gallery on the back of a hymn-book, and then painted the portrait on canvas at Cremyll boatyard. The churchyard

has interesting headstones, many of slate with their inscriptions clearly legible. An early form of cattle-grid keeps sheep and dogs out.

Turn right out of the churchyard to the footpath signposted to Empacombe and Cremyll Ferry and follow the path to a gate leading to the main road. Cross this to descend steps into Pigshill Wood. At times the path becomes vague, but try to keep to the most used track which descends steeply, often zigzagging. At the bottom go over a yellow-arrowed stile into a meadow, with the shore visible ahead. Cross the meadow diagonally, dropping to a gate on its north-east edge. Cross the road to continue on the footpath to Empacombe. Now there are lovely views of Millbrook Lake. The hedges in summer bear crops of sloes, and a curious tower of a derelict windmill is on the right. The path leads down to the quay at Empacombe. Follow the edge of the quay in front of the pink house to pass through the gate on its seaward side. The path now leads, with little difficulty, back to Cremyll, with the shore always close to the left. It emerges by the country park car park. ●

Cawsand

Looe, Kilminorth Wood and Talland Bay

Start	Entrance to Kilminorth Wood, West Looe
Distance	7 miles (11.25km)
Approximate time	3½ hours
Parking	Millpool car park, West Looe
Refreshments	Pubs and cafés at West Looe, café at Talland Bay, pub very near at Porthallow, tea-garden at Tencreek
Ordnance Survey maps	Landranger 201 (Plymouth) and Pathfinder 1355, SX 25/35 (Looe)

The descriptive notices about plants and birds on the first section through Kilminorth Wood certainly add to the enjoyment of a lovely creekside walk. The view of Talland on the descent from Tencreek is unforgettable, with the ancient tower of the church a foreground to the sweep of the bay. The walk back to Looe along the coastal path is enjoyable and undemanding.

From the top of the car park, take the Woodland Walk along the side of the river (not the bridleway which follows higher up). It is well worth reading the notices which describe the geology and wildlife. After about ½ mile (800m) by the shore, look for steps on the left (they are marked with a footpath arrow)

Talland Bay

which climb steeply to skirt the site of an old boatyard **Ⓐ** and cross the Giant's Hedge before dropping down the other side. The Hedge is an earthwork which runs from here to Lerryn, a distance of nearly 5 miles (8km). Tradition says that the Devil built it when he had nothing better to do, but it is rather more likely to have been a tribal defensive work. A path on the right allows access on to the saltmarsh as the river narrows.

At a picturesque group of houses, Watergate **Ⓑ**, turn left and make your way up the lane. A pleasant byway which is little used by traffic, this climbs steadily up through the wood by a stream. Halfway up the hill the bridleway

SCALE 1:27 777 or about 2¼ INCHES to 1 MILE 3.6CM to 1KM

| 0 | 200 | 400 | 600 | 800 METRES | 1 | |
| 0 | 200 | 400 | 600 YARDS | ½ | KILOMETRES MILES | |

through the upper woods meets it from the left. The wood ends before the large complex of holiday homes on the right (Kilminorth Farm Cottages) though the lane continues its long climb. Bear left with the made-up lane when it meets a farm track. At last the crest of the hill is reached and the view looking back can be enjoyed.

Cross the main road to the track to Waylands Farm. A lane on the right **C** goes to Tencreek Cottage tea-garden: follow it if refreshment is required; otherwise keep straight on, looking for a waymarked stile on the right to a camping field. Keep the hedge on the right here and follow the yellow waymark. Climb the stile on the right near the bottom of the field and cross the next field diagonally, aiming for a point close to where electricity cables cross over the hedge on the right. There is a gate here, near the bottom corner of the field.

The tower of Talland church can now be seen, but head instead just to the right of the Landmark **D**, one of two showing a measured nautical mile to ships on speed trials at sea. The diverted footpath passes over an improvised stile and down steep steps to a lane. Turn right down this to Talland church, worth visiting for its barrel roof and the carving on the bench ends. Note too the unusual, and sad, memorial to Joanna Mellow and her baby who died in childbirth in 1625. The carving on a slate slab in the floor at the east end of the church shows them both sitting up in a four-poster bed. The church has a covered way which serves as a porch and connects it to the detached tower.

From the church the lane descends steeply to Talland beach. There is a café here, or a short walk up the footpath to the left of the café brings you to the neighbouring village of Porthallow which has the Smugglers' Rest pub.

Cross the stile on to the coastal path, which after about $^{1}/_{2}$ mile (800m) enters the National Trust's Hendersick property. The path changes direction opposite the jagged Hore Stone and Bridge Rocks. Now the view to the east can be seen, with St George's Island offshore and the houses of Hannafore Point on the far side of Portnadler Bay. The other landmark is visible on the hilltop to the west of Hannafore. There is a healthy population of cormorants (or maybe shags) inhabiting the rocks below.

The coastal path is very distinct and well used here. Lovely Samphire Beach is reached by a stile at its eastern end. It is a pleasant place for a picnic even though it is rather close to the crowds at Looe.

At Hannafore the route follows the pavement on to the West Looe waterfront. There is a promenade by the river here to keep pedestrians away from the traffic. Go under the bridge to return to the car park and the starting point. ●

Looe

Around St Agnes

Start	Trevaunance Cove, St Agnes
Distance	5½ miles (8.75km) Shorter version 4½ miles (7.25km)
Approximate time	3 hours (2 hours for shorter version)
Parking	Car parks at Trevaunance Cove
Refreshments	Pub and café at Trevaunance Cove, also in St Agnes village
Ordnance Survey maps	Landranger 204 (Truro & Falmouth) and Pathfinder 1352, SW 75 (Perranporth)

Like most of these walks, there is much more to it than the distance given above implies. Some of the gradients are severe, but the scenery is constantly changing, and it is sobering to think that the miners who worked here in the 19th century had to climb these paths after a gruelling 16 or so hours underground. The walk can be shortened, if wished, after Ⓐ below.

Leave the car park and turn to the right to climb up the private road above the beach, passing the Trevaunance Cove Hotel on the seaward side. Go through the new-looking gate and then up the cliffside steps. The path is waymarked from this point. At the top of the steps the cliff path twists through the heather, past the remains of old tin workings. Just offshore are the jagged Bawden Rocks, more memorably known as 'Man and his Man'. The National Trust is the guardian of Newdowns Head from which there are lovely panoramas of Perran Bay with Newquay in the distance. On a clear day you will see Trevose Head on the far side of Newquay Bay. A footpath leads into the coastal path just before the National Trust sign Ⓐ.

At this point those lacking the time or inclination to tackle St Agnes Head and Beacon can turn left to walk along this footpath, later rejoining the main route at Ⓒ.

Continue along the coastal path and soon the coastguard lookout comes into view ahead, the path passing below it. Just beyond is St Agnes Head where the view to the west unfolds: the lighthouse on Godrevy Point can be seen on a decent day, with St Ives beyond. The rugged Carn Gowla Ⓑ is the western extremity of the walk: a picnic area and car park are sited on its landward side.

St Agnes

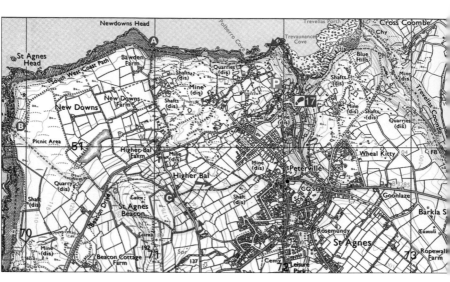

SCALE 1:29 412 or about 2¼ INCHES to 1 MILE 3.4CM to 1KM

```
0    200   400   600   800 METRES 1
                                   KILOMETRES
                                   MILES
0    200   400   600 YARDS   ½
```

Strike inland from here across the picnic area to head towards St Agnes Beacon (the cairn at its southern end is easily seen). A labyrinth of paths, as well as made-up roads, leads in the desired direction: it is best to aim for the cairn at this stage. A modern storage building will soon be seen ahead. The path to the beacon itself starts opposite this, on the other side of the road.

The beacon is cared for by the National Trust. If visibility is good bear to the right when the path divides to reach the summit – the view is magnificent. To avoid the climb, take the left-hand path which skirts the hill's northern flank. All routes meet again on the other, eastern, side of the beacon and lead on to a farm track descending towards St Agnes village. Turn left when this meets a road and 100 yds (92m) after the last house on the right look for a stone stile on the right with a path waymarked to Churchtown **C**. Keeping the stone wall on the left to the bottom of the field, use stone steps to climb the bank and cross the next field diagonally. The path is now easy to follow into the village. At Beaconsfield Place cross straight over to reach St Agnes Church and the main street. Turn left and then immediately right to take the Perranporth road, passing two pubs.

Follow the road for approximately ½ mile (800m) until you come to the Barkla Shop sign. Turn left here down a steep track **D** which has several 'sleeping policemen'. Turn right to cross over the stream by the footbridge, and then left to follow its left bank past Jericho Cottage.

This lovely section leads past a trout farm to the sea at Blue Hills, otherwise known as Trevellas Porth. It is a refreshing place to paddle, but bathing is dangerous at any time. The cove is overlooked by the dramatic ruins of engine-houses. Where the path meets the made-up road turn left and then right off the road at the hairpin bend to climb the footpath to the top of the cliff. This is the most arduous climb of the route, and soon afterwards you will see the beach of Trevaunance Cove below, the coastal path descending to the starting point by the Driftwood Spars Hotel. ●

Polkerris, Readymoney Cove and Gribbin Head

Start	Polkerris, a small cove to the west of Fowey
Distance	6½ miles (10.5km)
Approximate time	3 hours
Parking	Polkerris car park
Refreshments	Pub and café at Polkerris, café at Readymoney Cove
Ordnance Survey maps	Landranger 204 (Truro & Falmouth) and Pathfinder 1354, SX 05/15 (St Austell & Fowey)

Daphne du Maurier, author of Jamaica Inn *and* The Birds, *lived and wrote at Menabilly, the lovely estate which this route encircles. It is easy to see how she drew inspiration from these surroundings. The inland part of the walk is no less enjoyable than the clifftop section, and from Readymoney Cove there is a pleasant walk into town along the Fowey waterfront. It is possible to combine this route with Walk 5 (Polruan) by using the ferry across the river.*

Walk downhill from the car park towards the beach but before reaching it fork to the left past the post office and toilets and then left again by the

Readymoney Cove and the Fowey estuary

black and white building bearing the date 1912 (this looks as though it was once a fishermen's shelter but is now a holiday cottage). The coastal path climbs up the steps to the right but we keep straight on up a steep and narrow

path, worn down to the grooved bare rock.

Turn right at the road and then left after 200 yds (184m) **Ⓐ** (before the 'No Waiting' sign) following a path waymarked with the logo of the Saints' Way. Walk past Tregaminion farmhouse (unmistakable, as is its name in wrought iron above the church gateway) and bear right into the farmyard. Turn to the left by the tractor sheds and go through a gate into a field. Walk down to steps in the corner of the field, crossing a few boggy yards via the top of a conveniently-placed wall.

Keep the hedge on the right round the bottom of the next field to a Saints' Way sign pointing the way through an opening and over a stream. Now keep the hedge on the right again up the opposite side of the valley. There is a lovely view back over St Austell Bay from the top. Cross the stone stile before Trenant and follow the clearly-marked path past the sad, ruined farmyard on the right and up a gentle hill with the hedge on the left.

The stile at the top **Ⓑ** gives on to a steep path descending through the top end of Menabilly Wood. Pass under a bridge (it once took the main carriage drive to the mansion over the path) to another stile and stepping-stones at the bottom of the valley. The path runs up the other side of the valley with magnificent trees on the right.

There is a builder's yard at the top. Pass through the gate by a new house on to a lane and turn right. Carry straight on at the junction past a dead-end sign (or bear left for the quickest route to Fowey centre and the Polruan ferry). Turn left at the next junction, again following a Saints' Way sign. Now look for a National Trust track on the right, well marked as 'Love Lane, footpath to Readymoney' **Ⓒ**. This delightful, shady descent through Covington Woods is still part of the

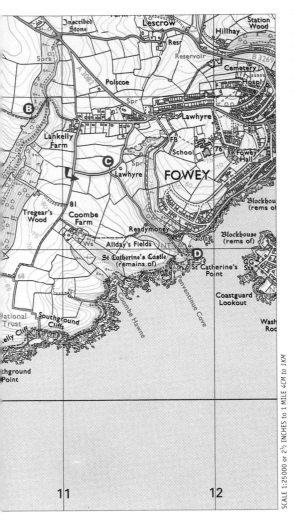

which were built on either side of the river with a chain stretched between them following the sacking of the town by the French in 1457.

Return to the trees to rejoin the coastal path – keep left and then right on the two occasions when the path divides to leave the woods and enter Alldays Fields. The tower on the top of Gribbin Head makes a fine landmark ahead. The route descends to the secluded beach at Coombe Haven which is weedy for a swim but is a good place to pause for a paddle or a picnic. There is a detour inland at the next cove, Polridmouth **E**, which was a part of the Menabilly Estate. This is a better place for a swim, but be careful: there are no lifeguards and the tides flow fast. From here there is a long, but not too steep, climb to Gribbin Head **F**. The 84-ft (25m) tower was erected in 1832 by Trinity House.

The final part of the route is enjoyable cliff walking. The peace may be slightly disturbed by the loud radios on the ships waiting offshore to load china clay at Par – they all seem to be tuned to Radio One. This is a level stretch which soon arrives at the trees fringing the Polkerris Valley. Keep these on the left. Where they end, turn sharply to the left to descend through them on a zigzagging path back to the starting place, passing both a pub and a café *en route*. ●

SCALE 1:25000 or 2½ INCHES to 1 MILE 4CM to 1KM

Saints' Way. The final part is on bare rock smoothed down by generations of pack animals: this is very slippery if wet. The path emerges on the shore of the Fowey River at Readymoney Cove, a delightful spot to linger – there is a café here (in the white house at the top of the slip) and the clear waters and sandy beach are refreshing for hot feet.

Leave the cove by the coastal path, climbing up the right-hand (western) side. At the top is St Catherine's Point **D**, a fine viewpoint. The castle here was built by Henry VIII to protect the entrance to the harbour. It supplemented two earlier blockhouses

Little Petherick Creek, Dennis Hill and the Camel Trail

Start	Little Petherick, south of Padstow
Distance	6 miles (9.5km)
Approximate time	3 hours
Parking	Little Petherick car park on west side of creek
Refreshments	Pubs and cafés in Padstow, café at Dennis Cove Holiday Park, pub at St Issey
Ordnance Survey maps	Landranger 200 (Newquay) and Pathfinder 1337, SW 87/97 (Padstow & Wadebridge)

The first part of the walk, along the west bank of the creek, is quite hard going at times, but there are many scenes of quiet beauty, as befits the Saints' Way. It is easy to make a detour into Padstow, and an alternative return to Little Petherick (from point Ⓓ *below) is offered, as at certain times of the year the fields west of Trevilgus Farm may be under cultivation, which might necessitate long detours around their edges.*

From the car park at Little Petherick turn right to walk down the creek along a drive to holiday chalets. Once past these the path climbs above the creek through trees. A stile and steps lie ahead, and beyond these there are fine views over the river. The trees are lovely here and in autumn the colours must be spectacular.

A stile takes the path out of the wood and into a meadow. Note the wonderfully constructed wall on the left. Follow the Saints' Way sign with the wall on the left until at the top of the hill you see an avenue of ash trees on the right. Follow these above a wooded combe to an ancient sunken track (one can well imagine a file of robed figures trudging up here). This leads down to the river. Cross the pill (inlet) by a footbridge at its head and then climb up again on the other side. At the top there is a fine view to the River Camel, with the monument on Dennis Hill prominent.

Keep the river on the right, heading for the monument. Note Sea Mills below, with its tidal wall which was used for harnessing the power of the tides. Another inlet forces a diversion from the direct route (the map says it is possible to cross at low tide but it would be a very muddy business). When you come to an inviting-looking stile near the bottom, do not cross it but instead turn right and make your way towards a wooden post which stands near steps leading to the bottom of the pill (the waymarking here is only for southbound walkers).

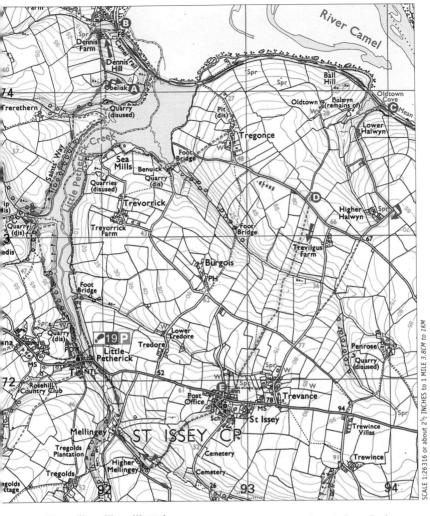

SCALE 1:26 316 or about 2½ INCHES to 1 MILE 3.8CM to 1KM

0   200   400   600   800 METRES   1
0   200   400   600 YARDS   ½

KILOMETRES
MILES

Having skirted the head of the small creek climb up the side of the valley again to reach a meadow. The obelisk can be clearly seen now; climb to the top of the meadow to reach it. Erected to commemorate Queen Victoria's Jubilee in 1887, it is a magnificent viewpoint **A**.

Returning from the short path that leads to the monument, follow the left edge of the field to reach a gate and concrete stile at the bottom. Turn left and then right on to a made-up road through Dennis Cove Leisure Park (there is a café in the complex, by the swimming-pool). A footpath leads through the leisure park, to the left of a small lake, to reach the old railway track which is now the Camel Trail **B**. Turn left on to the trail for an easy ten-minute walk into Padstow, or right to continue on the walk. In either case, beware of bicycle traffic along the trail: cyclists are meant to give way to walkers, but the trail often resembles the Tour de France here. The trail has not been made a right of way, as the council feels that it is easier to solve problems like this if it retains control.

The Camel Trail can be walked to Wadebridge and beyond, even to Bodmin. As it follows the old railway line, the gradients are virtually non-existent and the scenery splendid.

To return to Little Petherick, cross the fine railway bridge over the creek and follow the trail by the side of the Camel to a bridge over Oldtown Creek **C**. Having crossed this, leave the Camel Trail and climb a track which becomes a made-up lane at the top. Turn right here (do not take the footpath straight ahead) and after the turn to Trevilgus look for a footpath heading towards St Issey church on the left **D**.

There is, however, a choice here. If the next two or three fields are cropped,

Padstow

and there have not been enough walkers to mark a footpath through them, it will be easier for you to return on the east side of Little Petherick creek. This is quite straightforward. Keep to the road towards Tregonce, but before reaching the farm fork left on a track leading to the river. Just before this track reaches the shore take a footpath on the left which leads alongside the creek back to Little Petherick. The only possible difficulty with this variation would be if an unusually high tide blocked access beyond Sea Mills.

The St Issey footpath crosses four fields directly, the descent over the last two being steep. Use the stepping-stones to cross the stream and then head uphill, crossing a big field to find a new stile. Head for the top right-hand corner of the next field to reach the lane. Cross this and climb up steps into another field.

Continue heading for St Issey church, now that you can see it again, crossing a stream and then a stone stile on the right-hand side of the following field. The path emerges on to the main road opposite the church **E**, with the Ring o' Bells pub on the right.

St Issey was a female Irish saint born in 480 and descended from one of the early High Kings. Baptised Daidre, she took the name Itha 'on account of her thirst for the living water of Heavenly Truth'. The church was rebuilt in 1870 after the tower fell, though a few items, including the font, from the old building survive.

Leave the church on its south side (by the school) and turn right into the lane. Take the path on the left through the farmyard (the sign is by a white garage door opposite). After the farmyard keep the hedge on the right to pass through a gate at the narrow end of an abutting field. Now keep the hedge on the right again heading steeply down to a bridge and stepping-stones at the bottom. Climb to a stile in the wall on the right and walk through an abandoned farmyard to reach the lane at Higher Melingey. Turn right down this and after the mill take the path on the left which follows the valley to emerge, through a gate, on to the main road above Little Petherick. ●

Portloe and Veryan

Start	Carne Beach near Veryan, between St Mawes and Mevagissey
Distance	7 miles (11.25km)
Approximate time	4 hours
Parking	Carne Beach car park
Refreshments	Pubs and cafés at Portloe and Veryan
Ordnance Survey maps	Landranger 204 (Truro & Falmouth) and Pathfinder 1366, SW 83/73/93 (Falmouth & St Mawes)

This is just about the perfect walk for a family. The outward leg along the coastal path is as exhilarating as it is exhausting, with wonderful views of the coastline in each direction. Portloe is reached at just the right moment for welcome rest and refreshment. The walk to Veryan is along lanes and through fields, the last a beautiful recreation ground by the church. The swings and see-saw will revive children beginning to flag.

Leave the car park and turn to the left on to the lane in front of the beach. Where this bends to the left away from the sea look for steps on the right up the bank to a kissing-gate giving on to the cliff path. Even from this early point there is a splendid view southwards over Gerrans Bay. Below the cliffs great numbers of shags (or cormorants) sit and preen themselves on the rocks or dive into the sea hunting for fish. At Tregagle's Hole keep on the cliff path, climbing the steep hill.

According to legend, Tregagle was a lawyer who returned from the grave to torment a man who had wronged him. Having successfully resisted many attempts at exorcism, his spirit was at last laid in Gwenvor Cove, given the chore of making a truss of sand,

bound round with ropes of the same material. In times of storm he may be heard roaring with frustration at this hopeless task, which he will still be attempting on Judgement Day. (Note that 'truss', in this context, is not a medical support but a tied-up bundle of hay or straw.)

Do not be tempted by paths on the seaward side which twist through the

Portloe

PORTLOE AND VERYAN ● 57

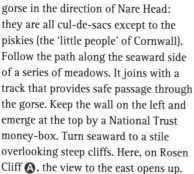

gorse in the direction of Nare Head:
they are all cul-de-sacs except to the
piskies (the 'little people' of Cornwall).
Follow the path along the seaward side
of a series of meadows. It joins with a
track that provides safe passage through
the gorse. Keep the wall on the left and
emerge at the top by a National Trust
money-box. Turn seaward to a stile
overlooking steep cliffs. Here, on Rosen
Cliff **A**, the view to the east opens up.

Cross the sheep fence by the stile in
the corner of the field and descend to
Kiberick Cove, taking note of the notice
which reads 'Footpath runs round the

head of valley and along fence to stile'.
The thickness of gorse at the top of the
field makes this impossible, however, so
cut across the valley to reach the fence
by a gate and then follow the path
along, with crops on one side and the
sea on the other. In August there was a
host of butterflies here, pale blue
commas as well as tortoiseshells. The
path ascends in zigzags to reach a white
house at the top. Here the path bends
seaward again after another National
Trust money-box, through a lovely
planting of pine trees. As the coastal
path begins its descent into Portloe
those not wishing to visit the village
may make use of the path on the left **B**
which by-passes Portloe.

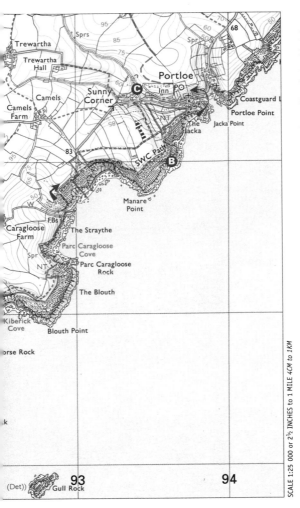

lane. Go through a number of metal gates and walk straight across the field to a stone stile set in a fence by trees. Go through this narrow belt of trees to a gate on the far side. Cross the next meadow diagonally, heading down towards the tower of Veryan church, half-hidden by trees. The stone stile by the stream at the bottom of the field leads into one of the loveliest recreation grounds in the country **D**, with swings, roundabout and see-saw. Walk through this, with the stream and then the church on the left and the pond on the right. On the road turn left passing the New Inn on the left. Take the St Mawes road out of the village, climbing up the hill towards the sports centre. Pass this on the

SCALE 1:25 000 or 2½ INCHES to 1 MILE 4CM to 1KM

The path descends to the slipway; turn left here and climb the hill past the post office, bearing left to pass the Ship Inn. Continue along the road, which passes over one stream and alongside another, to find the footpath to Veryan on the right **C**. This leads past Old White Cottage and some newer properties to a gate into a meadow. Cross to the right side of the meadow and climb the wall by the yellow arrows. Now keep the wall on the left to the gate at the top of the field. Here there is a short enclosed cattle-track. Turn right at the farmyard on to the made-up track to Trewartha.

Turn left at the T-junction and then immediately right past the Methodist church and along an enclosed grassy

left and ignore the footpath on the other side going to Ruan High Lanes. Now the road descends steeply, becoming narrow and banked. The ruined mill at Melinsey is picturesque; its paddles have gone but the cast-iron wheel remains.

At the sharp bend take the footpath straight ahead to Pendower Beach. This begins with a steep ascent up the side of the valley, but then descends through trees. Cross the bridge over the stream at the bottom and continue through the grounds of Lower Mill to the footpath on the left side of the stream. This is a short walk to the car park at Pendower Beach. Turn left, either along the beach or on the access road if the tide is up, to reach the starting point at Carne. ●

Chûn Quoit, Pendeen Watch and Botallack

Start	Carnyorth, north of St Just
Distance	8 miles (12.75km)
Approximate time	4½ hours
Parking	By the school at Carnyorth, opposite a telephone-box
Refreshments	Restaurant (closed Mondays) and pub at Botallack
Ordnance Survey maps	Landranger 203 (Land's End) and Explorer 7 (Land's End)

This is a fine way to explore the unique character of the far west of Cornwall. The first leg of the walk climbs up to wild moorland which is a perfect setting for one of the most evocative of Penwith's antiquities, Chûn Quoit. The next section takes in a wild stretch of coastline, and finally there is the chance to see the mines that brought prosperity to the area 150 years ago. Do not attempt this walk in bad visibility.

Cross the main road and head up the lane towards the radio mast, passing to the left of the house at the top and crossing a stile (with an orange waymark). Keep heading towards the mast across two meadows, and after the second continue along a path leading through bracken. There is a fine view back as the mast is approached and the path meets a track. Cross this to another track that goes to the mast. From here there is an impressive view of Carn Kenidjack, which on a misty morning rather resembles St Michael's Mount. Follow the path that leads to the left of this tor, passing an ancient milestone on the left and with the strange shape of the air traffic control station in the distance. This is a lovely moorland walk as the path becomes narrow through an overgrown enclosure before emerging on to another farm track.

Cross over the road, following the Tinners' Way sign. Chûn Quoit – a neolithic tomb – can be seen to the left of the summit of the hill ahead. Bear to the left when the path forks **Ⓐ**, towards the quoit which is hidden from view until the last moment – if in doubt head to the left of the summit.

There are wonderful views all round from the quoit, and even better ones if you make the short climb up to the castle **Ⓑ**. There was an Iron Age village within the ramparts of the stronghold.

Returning to the quoit head north and begin to descend, with the ancient hedge (and, in the distance, Morvah church) on the left. The path leads off the moor and narrows. Eventually it joins a track, which in turn joins with another; bear left here and continue downhill. At the next track-junction head towards Carne Farm; Morvah church is again on the left at this point.

Chûn Quoit

Before you reach the farmyard there is a footpath sign on the left pointing across a field. This may be closely cropped and without a headland, in which case a detour may be necessary. After this head across the fields directly towards Morvah church, finally crossing the main road to reach it **C**.

The path to the cliffs is on the right of the church, steps leading over the wall. This is a romantic path that twists down to the sea, and one can well imagine villagers charging down here with their lanterns on a stormy night when a ship was in peril off-shore. At the end of a broad enclosure climb the wall to the right to reach the coastal footpath **D**. Turn left and walk along a level path. The best views are in the other direction, of precipitous Trevowhan and Trevean cliffs, beloved of rock climbers.

As the path drops down to Portheras, Pendeen lighthouse can be seen ahead.

An unusual environmental hazard has afflicted Portheras, which was once a delightful and relatively undiscovered bathing cove with a smooth sandy beach. A ship wrecked here many years ago is now being ground down into fragments by the remorseless breakers, with the result that the sand hides a million razor-sharp pieces of steel, some quite large but most very small. Notices warn people not to bathe or go barefoot on the sands. However, it would seem to be harmless to bathe aching feet in the clear stream that rushes down to the sea here, and is crossed by stepping stones.

It is a steep climb out of Portheras, going up to Pendeen Watch **E**, where a beacon warned shipping of the dangerous headland before the lighthouse was built. Visitors are welcome to inspect Pendeen lighthouse. This stretch of coastline claimed a vast tonnage of shipping even after the opening of the lighthouse (the total of 34 ships being more than the combined

0	200	400	600	800 METRES	1
					KILOMETRES
					MILES
0	200	400	600 YARDS	½	

total for the Manacles, Lizard and Runnelstone, according to Larn and Carter in *Cornish Shipwrecks*). Nearly all the wrecks were of colliers engaged in trading to and from the coalfields of South Wales. Shipwreck was often quick, and, just occasionally, painless. When the *Umbre* of Cork went down off

Greeb Point on 20 February, 1899 (when the lighthouse was being built) it was all over in a few minutes. The captain, two officers, a stewardess, nine crewmen, the ship's dog, cat and parrot were all rescued and having breakfast at the Commercial Hotel, St Just, by 8am, hardly more than two hours after their ship had hit the rocks.

From the lighthouse the view ahead is impressive, with the remains of old

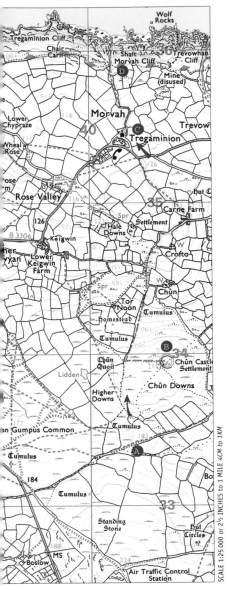

SCALE 1:25 000 or 2½ INCHES to 1 MILE 4CM to 1KM

right opposite the end of the terrace. The path winds through the ruins of the Levant Mine where even the buildings are stained red. The settling beds are still full of red mud and a bridge takes the path across a stream that carries the waste from Geevor to the sea. An interesting feature to the right is the Levant beam-engine which has been restored and is now under the care of the National Trust. It is open to the public at times in the summer, and is occasionally fired up and run so visitors can see it in action.

Should you feel in need of refreshment at this point, a notice by the beam-engine advertises a tea shop 300 yds (274m) up the lane; this would be near Trewellard, and from there a footpath takes you back to the starting point at Carnyorth.

But the best bet is to nurse the thirst and keep on the coastal footpath, passing the triangulation pillar on the right and a house called Roscommon on the left. Now there is a grand view of Cape Cornwall ahead, but look down and to the right as well. There, tucked into the bottom of the cliffs, is the most romantic of all ruined engine-houses, Botallack **F**. The shafts of this mine extended far out under the sea.

We leave the coastal footpath here, keeping on the track past modern lifting gear on the left (Allen's Shaft). The lane heads towards St Just, passing the Count House and the lovely Manor Farm. From here an excellent pub, the Queen's Arms, is straight on.

Retrace a few steps after the pub, turning right at Little Fasily (but left, of course, if you have decided against visiting the pub). Pass the telephone box on the main road, and then turn left **G** through a gap in a line of cottages to a stone stile. Keep the wall on the left and head for the school to return to the starting point. ●

engine-houses testifying to the district's importance in the heyday of tin-mining early in the 19th century. The redness of the sea shows that a small part of that industry survives – this is waste from Geevor Mine.

Climb up the road from the lighthouse towards the terrace of Trinity House cottages. Note the curious watch-tower in the end house and be ready to turn off the road to the

Dizzard Point, St Gennys and Millook Water

Dizzard Point, St Gennys and Millook Water

Start	Cancleave near Millook, south-west of Bude
Distance	7 miles (11.25km)
Approximate time	4½ hours
Parking	Parking space for Cancleave Strand, 1 mile (1.5km) south-west of Millook
Refreshments	Pub and café at Crackington Haven, only a short diversion from the route
Ordnance Survey maps	Landranger 190 (Bude & Clovelly) and Pathfinder 1310, SX 19 (St Gennys)

There can be few more energetic sections of the North Coast Path than this, and few that are less trodden. But the walking here is exhilarating, and the steep climbs all seem worth while when a pause is made to take in the view. Only a very short part of the walk uses a road carrying much traffic, and the final section passes through a rare example of Cornwall's primeval woodland.

As you drive south-west from Millook keep a watch for a cottage on the right called Cancleave. The parking spaces are on the other side of the road, where a footpath crosses. Use the stile on the seaward side of the road opposite the car park to reach a path which joins the coastal footpath within a few yards. Turn left here, but first look back towards Millook to see an example of the geological folding for which this area is famous.

Unusually, the path follows the edge of the cliff on unworn grass. It skirts the side of a wooded combe before plunging into it. The trees are mainly stunted oaks, well beaten by the gales. A bridge crosses a stream at the bottom and then the path climbs steeply to reach Bynorth Cliff. There is a fine view back across Widemouth Bay. This would be a taxing walk in a strong

SCALE 1:31250 or 2 INCHES to 1 MILE 3.2CM to 1KM

westerly. There is a triangulation pillar above Dizzard Point with a spot-height of 538ft (164m). Soon after this look for a stile where the scrub ends; this leads the path to the cliff edge. The view to the east is even better. The cliff-edge vegetation is now of stunted oaks with a few examples of gorse, which always seems to be able to show a flower even in the bleakest months.

The first great test of stamina is now to be faced. At Chipman Point **A** the path plunges down a precipitous cliff-face (up to now the cliffs, though high, have been gently-sloping). Note the contorted strata far below, and the daunting climb up the opposite side of this valley. Fortunately steps have been made up much of it. The stream descends to the shore as a waterfall. At the top the tower of St Gennys church can be seen peeping above the flank of the hill. Another steep descent/ascent soon follows, though not as severe as the previous one. Quite close to us on the left is the farmhouse of Cleave and the scant remains of the medieval village of Tresmorn – a few grassy hillocks may be seen.

From Cleave the path goes right out on to the headland before dropping down to the valley. This is National Trust land. It is possible to glimpse Boscastle from here, beyond Cambeak which guards the entrance to Crackington Haven. The steep climb up the southern side of this valley is unassisted by steps; it must be very tricky to descend in wet weather. At the top **B** pause to regain breath and admire the view of Cambeak and Crackington Haven. If you need refreshment it is easy to walk down to the village from here, but the climb back would be severe. Study of the map will show less arduous ways of regaining the route, though probably at the expense of missing St Gennys.

If you do not want to go into the village keep to the route by crossing the stile and follow the fence inland to another stile. Now a traditional stone hedge is on the left, and this accompanies the path to the village of St Gennys, with the church a perfect foreground to a panorama of farmland and coastline. The church is a quiet and beautiful place to rest. St Genny was St Genesius, who according to tradition was beheaded and walked about with his head beneath his arm.

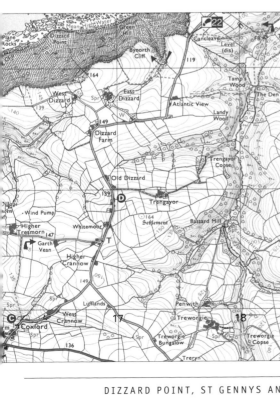

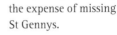

Leave the church and take the road past the Old School House, following it to the main Crackington road (where those who sought refreshment would probably rejoin the route). Continue to a junction by a white-washed Methodist church, and turn left to Coxford. At the bottom of the steep hill **⊙**, just before Coxford Cottage, cross the footbridge on the left and then climb up the steepest part of the meadow northwards to find a gate in the wall bearing a footpath sign. Keep the hedge on the right after this, still climbing, though less strenuously now. There are fine views from here over the countryside covered earlier. The path reaches an enclosed lane which leads to the road coming from Tresmorn; turn right on to this.

When this byway reaches the lane to Millook by a telephone-box turn left, and follow it for about ¼ mile (400m) to a white bungalow on the right, where the drive to Trengayor meets the road **⊙**. Walk along this drive and through the farmyard to a muddy track on the other side. After a new metal gate across this, find another gate on the left bearing a Woodland Trust logo, with footpath waymarking close by. Take this path to enter one of

Cornwall's finest primeval woods. Beware of the brambles and nettles which encroach on the path in places. The abundance of small birds emphasises the value of this sort of environment. The trees are mainly tall, thin oaks, often with ferns growing from their branches, but there are many other indigenous species, most notably holly. The footpath descends steadily and at the bottom divides. Take the left fork and cross the stream.

The path follows the left bank of the stream which would seem to be an ideal habitat for kingfishers. A white house appears through the trees with a footbridge opposite. Cross this and the somewhat muddy meadow beyond to pass behind the house. At the end of its drive there is a bridge over an electric fence which takes the path into a meadow. Notice that the meadow supports many of the wild flowers that used to flourish in such places before herbicides. At the end of the meadow the fence is again bridged, and then the path enters the wood again. The stream (Millook Water) is now on the left.

The next landmark to be seen is a charming thatched cottage at Trebarfoote Coombe. Cross the footbridge before reaching it and look for a very modest unwaymarked footpath on the left, which climbs on the left bank of a streamlet. Eventually a gate is reached, and after this continue to follow the left side of the valley to a stile. This is a good point at which to pause and look back at the countryside. There is a steep final ascent before the road is reached by the parking place at Cancleave. ●

St Gennys

Lizard Point, Kynance Cove and Cadgwith

Start	Lizard Point
Distance	8 miles (12.75km)
Approximate time	4 hours
Parking	The Most Southerly Point, or the car park by the lighthouse
Refreshments	Cafés and pubs at Lizard Point and Cadgwith, seasonal café at Kynance Cove
Ordnance Survey maps	Landrangers 203 (Land's End) and 204 (Truro & Falmouth), Explorer 8 (The Lizard)

It looks quite a short distance on the map but this is deceptive, as the coastal path is exceptionally tortuous, though without severe gradients. The scenery is outstanding, especially if a rough sea is running, and the inland leg makes a pleasant contrast with the coastal sections.

At Lizard Point, the most southerly point of Britain, turn right on to the coastal footpath. From the first headland **A** there is a fine view back to the squat lighthouse and the point. The colouring of the rocks of the Lizard is very distinctive; they lack the pinkish hue of those of the Land's End peninsula. They have evocative names such as Man of War, Barges Rock, the Stags and Shag Rock. All have played their part in claiming lives, and 207 were drowned when the *Royal Anne* was wrecked on the Stags in November, 1720. The victims were buried on the clifftop in Pistol Meadow, Polpeor.

Shipwreck occasionally had its lighter moments. When about fifty years later a Quebec-registered ship sailing for Hull hit the same reef the crew were able to scramble on to Crenvil Rock. The light of dawn showed one man clutching a large cask, and

another desperately holding on to a live pig. When the crew staggered ashore they were met by the ship's cat which had also survived at the cost of half of its tail. They made a strange procession as they marched into the village, where they were able to drink the nine gallons of rum that the cask contained, and trade the pig for the price of a ride to Falmouth. The ginger cat was presented to the landlord of the inn, where it led a contented life until it died of old age.

From Old Lizard Head the view ahead opens up with the shapes of the rock stacks of Kynance in the distance ahead. The crowds will now have thinned out and there is springy level turf to walk on. Almost too soon the National Trust's car park for Kynance Cove comes into view. The Trust has an excellent leaflet on the history, human and natural, of the cove. This was one of the places beloved by the

'Excursionists' of the 19th century. Prince Albert brought his children ashore here in 1846, and Tennyson paid his first visit to the cove two years later. It was the Victorians who were responsible for giving the various features of the area such fanciful names – where did the inspiration for Asparagus Island come from?

Having admired the beauty spot **B** from afar and close to, and perhaps pausing for refreshment at the café (which operates quite a short season, closing before the end of September), take the track which follows the valley, labelled 'Return path to car park avoiding steps'. Fork to the left off this, when the track levels out after zigzags, along a broad, well-trodden path which strikes in a fairly straight line across the heath. The heather, *Erica vagans*, is unique to this small part of Britain. You are now walking at the top of the valley and parallel to it.

Ignore the signpost showing a footpath to the left but continue to head for a row of houses in the distance. The constant buzzing of helicopters may be an irritation, but they seem to work to office hours. The final part of the path before the road can be muddy, some of the mud having a strange golden colour.

Cross the road **C** to a track on the opposite side (at the left end of the row of houses mentioned earlier). This soon becomes a path made narrow and low by the encroachment of brambles and gorse. This is a short section, though, and it soon opens into a lovely heathy wilderness with the tower of St Grade's Church ahead (more correctly, St Grada of the Holy Cross). Another short

SCALE 1:25 000 or 2½ INCHES to 1 MILE 4CM to 1KM

Leave the churchyard at the eastern end over a stone stile. Keep the wall on the left to the bottom right-hand corner of the field, where an enclosed path leads to the road. Cross the road to a white house, Metheven, and pass this on your right to follow the lane towards Inglewidden (the name is on an old stone gatepost). Bear to the left at the junction for the Devil's Frying-pan. Note how the trees here have died: this has greatly marred the beauty of Cadgwith. Where the lane branches to the right **E** you can keep straight on to visit Cadgwith, following the coastal footpath sign (you will have to retrace your steps to this point), but the route returning to the Lizard turns right following the sign for Inglewidden. Keep straight on past Town Place, a National Trust cottage, to the end of its field, a National Trust car park. Follow the sign to the Devil's Frying-pan

section of enclosed path, deeply rutted by hoofed traffic (this is a bridleway) leads to the road.

Turn right and keep straight on at the junction, heading for Grade. Take the track on the left to the church **D**, which in summer is left unlocked – a place of tranquillity. There is no electric power here and for services the church is lit by oil lamps and the organ bellows pumped by hand.

to find it immediately below, a spectacular natural feature of a rock arch below sheer cliffs which curve like a basin around it. You are now on the coastal footpath again, heading south.

The subsequent going along the coastal path is straightforward, if energetic. The Lizard is in view ahead. The curiously shaped rock just before Studio Golva would seem to be more chair-like than the feature of that name later on. The church that gives its name to Church Cove nestles amongst trees and buildings on the right as the path dips down to the cove. A sign says that this was bought for the National Trust by the Caravan Club, which seems ironic in view of the way caravan sites have blighted so much of our coastline.

Climbing the cliff on the other side there is a wonderful view back to Cadgwith and beyond. The path passes behind the lifeboat station and in front of the coastguards' lookout on Bass Point **F**. Just beyond this is a white castellated building which was the Lloyds Signal Station. Before the electric telegraph and efficient signalling apparatus this was of great importance as ships had to sail close in to the dangerous shore in order to send or receive vital signals (which were small squares of bunting hung from a mast). Pen Olver is the rocky headland to the left as the path follows a stone hedge past an old bungalow. Note the bronze plaque here, celebrating the work of Guglielmo Marconi, who used the building for his pioneering work on wireless telegraphy.

The lighthouse comes into view ahead. A stop for refreshment can be made at the Housel Bay Hotel before a last climb leads up the cliffs to the car park by the Lizard lighthouse. ●

Lizard Point

Zennor to St Ives by the Tinners' Way

Start	Zennor
Distance	8½ miles (13.5km). Shorter version 5 miles (8km)
Approximate time	4½ hours (2½ hours for shorter version)
Parking	Car park at Zennor
Refreshments	Tinners Arms pub at Zennor
Ordnance Survey maps	Landranger 203 (Land's End) and Explorer 7 (Land's End)

A fine walk along one of the most spectacular parts of the Cornish coast. The inland section is hardly less enjoyable, a clearly marked path linking farmsteads, each about ½ mile (800m) apart. Many of the small fields, and their stone hedges, date from prehistoric times. Although some of the inland path is labelled as a part of the Tinners' Way, it is known locally as the Coffin Path. The coastal path lives up to its name, often dipping down almost to the shoreline before soaring up again to the clifftop. The walk can be shortened after point Ⓐ below.

The path starts at the western end of the churchyard. There is a gate between the wall of the churchyard and a barn which leads to a meadow with a path alongside the wall on the left. It is a very easy path to follow, as it progresses in a more-or-less straight line over a series of stone stiles and cattle-grids which are easily seen ahead. If in doubt head for the next farmstead. From Tremedda follow the electricity lines and at Tregerthen go to the right of the farm to a narrow enclosed path which still follows the electricity line quite closely. After this point the stiles are clearly marked by striped posts.

Pass through the farmyard at Wicca. A sign shows the field occupied by 'The BULL', but luckily it is kept well away from our path. Follow the farm track to

Boscubben Ⓐ, and after the farm take the track to the left.

Those wishing only to do the shorter version of the walk can follow this track towards the coastal path, rejoining the main route there Ⓓ.

After about 50 yds (46m) the main route branches off the track to the

From Zennor Head

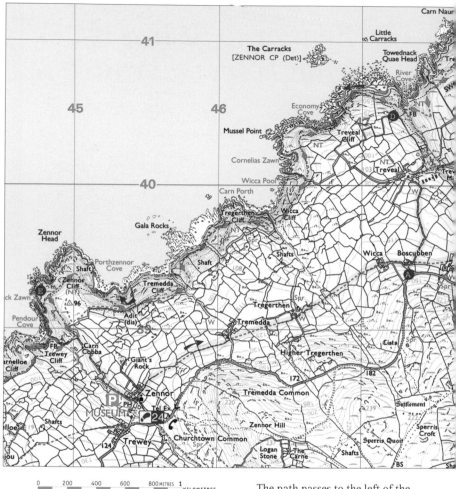

0	200	400	600	800 METRES	1
0	200	400	600 YARDS	½	KILOMETRES MILES

right, over a stone stile marked by a striped pole.

At Trendrine there is a Tinners' Way routemark. Pass through the farmyard with the house on the right. Then head for the next house, Trevessa, across the field. At Trevessa turn left on to the lane and then immediately right by Little Trevega. Head for a modern-looking house at the top through the next long meadow and pass to the right of it, following electricity wires to find the next waymark. Climb the stile into the lane, turn right, and after 200 yds (184m) turn left, following Tinners' Way signs. Trevalgan is the next farm.

The path passes to the left of the farm, and the next farmstead, Trowan, is in a straight line ahead. Carry straight on from here too, still following the clearly marked path that has led us from farm to farm from Zennor, until the path arrives at a farm track which is a footpath crossroads **B**. If you wish to visit St Ives go straight on here – it is about half an hour's walk but be warned that it involves a steep climb back to the coastal footpath which is joined at the western end of Porthmeor Beach.

Our route, however, omits St Ives, instead turning left along the track to join the coastal footpath on Hellesveor Cliff **C**. Turn westwards (to the left) after admiring the view eastwards

SCALE 1:26 316 or about 2½ INCHES to 1 MILE 4CM to 1KM

across St Ives Bay to Godrevy lighthouse and beyond.

There is an even better view back from the next headland – Pen Enys – where planks are laid so that the worst of the mud at the valley bottom is avoided. The spot-height marked at the triangulation pillar on Trevega Cliff is 300ft (91m). After this the view opens up westwards to Pendeen lighthouse. Strangely there is no point where you can get views of a lighthouse in each direction: Godrevy to the east, and Pendeen west. Just beyond River Cove a path joins from Treveal: this is the shorter alternative route **D**.

From the next headland, Mussel Point, the view to Zennor and Gurnard's headlands is even better.

After Tregerthen this is a true coastal footpath – now plunging to the shoreline, the next moment high up on the cliffs above, and usually twisting and turning through a scattering of enormous boulders.

You may think that you have reached Zennor Head when you have climbed up to the rock tower that overlooks Porthzennor Cove, but this is a false summit. You have to walk to the next tor **E**, which has a plaque on it, to find the true Zennor Head. The views from both prominences are equally spectacular, however.

The path back to the village follows the valley, soon joining a lane which leads both to the church and (oh joy!) the Tinners Arms. ●

Trebarwith and Delabole

Trebarwith and Delabole

Start	Trebarwith Strand
Distance	9 miles (14.5km) Shorter version 5½ miles (8.75km)
Approximate time	5½ hours (3 hours for shorter version)
Parking	Trebarwith
Refreshment	Pub and bistro at Trebarwith, cafés and pubs at Delabole (though off the route)
Ordnance Survey maps	Landranger 200 (Newquay & Bodmin) and Explorer 9 (Bodmin Moor)

Although the distance is given as only 9 miles (14.5km), this is deceptive. The opening section is very energetic – a delightful switchback leading into remote and beautiful coves. The field sections come as a relief after the previous gradients, and the views of open countryside are delightful. The route continues round the rim of England's largest hole in the ground – the great slate quarry at Delabole, and then returns to Trebarwith via a quiet country byway. This is not a walk for a very windy day. It can be shortened, if wished, after point ❶ below.

The lane which leads down to Trebarwith Strand follows one of Cornwall's most spectacular valleys. At the seaward end is the former Trebarwith Strand Hotel, and by it the coastal path begins its formidable climb up to the cliffs on the southern side of the cove. It passes to the left of the Port William pub and soon the gradient becomes severe, though the steps make the climbing safe, if liable to leave walkers a little breathless.

The view from Dennis Point is fabulous – Tintagel in the near distance to the north, Gull Rock just offshore, and, to the south, the gentle sweep of Port Isaac Bay lined with a series of precipitous cliffs. However, linger only long enough to regain breath for the next part of the switchback, zigzagging down to the bridges at Backways Cove.

Again the climb on the other side is steep, but the views from the top, Treligga Cliff, are the reward. More of Port Isaac Bay is revealed, and Pentire Point can be seen if visibility is reasonable. An easy level stretch of clifftop walking follows. At first the cliffs are nearly vertical, but they become less precipitous as Tregonnick Point is approached. Here the path descends gently by The Mountain ❶ to a signpost.

At this point, those who would prefer to do the shorter version of the walk can take a short cut to Delabole via Tregardock and Treligga Downs (where there is a pub).

You may enjoy a diversion here to Tregardock Beach (though this is not worthwhile at high tide) where the sand is smooth and the beach is often deserted and without footprints – a lovely place to picnic or paddle, but take care of the smoothed steps leading down to the sand.

The main route continues along the coastal path. Climbing back to the clifftop, it is a relief again to find that a level stretch follows. Just before Jacket's Point a notice warns that the clifftop is cracked, so walk well inland. There is a lovely view of Port Isaac. Landslips here have left curious landforms, some almost like cliff dwellings. There is also strange terracing inland as the path descends to Jacket's Point where a lovely waterfall drops to a rocky cove. There is also a sinister cave.

Another steep climb follows, with steps up the final 50ft (15m). Pause to enjoy the view from the top, for we will shortly be leaving the coast to take to the fields. Just before the look-out **B** take the stile on the left and follow the wall towards a ruined farm. Go straight through the abandoned farmyard to a track on the far side. When this divides, carry straight on rather than bearing to the right towards asbestos farm buildings. Where the footpath bends to the left the way may still be obstructed by an old trailer blocking the gateway –

Trebarwith Strand

an easy obstacle to surmount. Go through or over the next gate (the white Tregragon Farm is on the left) and then climb the gate immediately on the right and cross the field diagonally. There is a gate and a stile at the top right-hand corner of this large field. Now keep the hedge on the right to reach an enclosed track which leads to a ramshackle farmyard and then to the road. There is a footpath signpost at this end – the only one to be seen.

Turn left on to the road: unfortunately the footpath that soon appears on the right is blocked by barbed wire close to a steep bank, so we have to continue on the road past the three junctions at Westdowns – the last one, to Treligga, leads to a pub after ½ mile (800m) – to a driveway to Delamere Holiday Village on the right, just before the 40mph sign **C**.

This track crosses the old railway and passes in front of the old farmhouse of Delamere which now services the holiday chalets in its grounds. A stile on the far side of the lawn (with a log cabin on the left) leads into a field. Cross this to find a gate at the bottom. There is a disused stile here with a very old thorn tree grown through it. Cross a stream and keep the hedge on the right to the next gate, into Helland Barton farmyard **D**. Turn left up the drive.

At the first junction bear right (don't continue uphill) along a track. (There is an alternative here if preferred: a footpath follows parallel to the track through the meadow on the left.) Bear to the right when the track emerges in Delabole, past old quarrymen's cottages, and then right again to enter the quarry, where there is a public viewing area to allow inspection of England's largest hole in the ground.

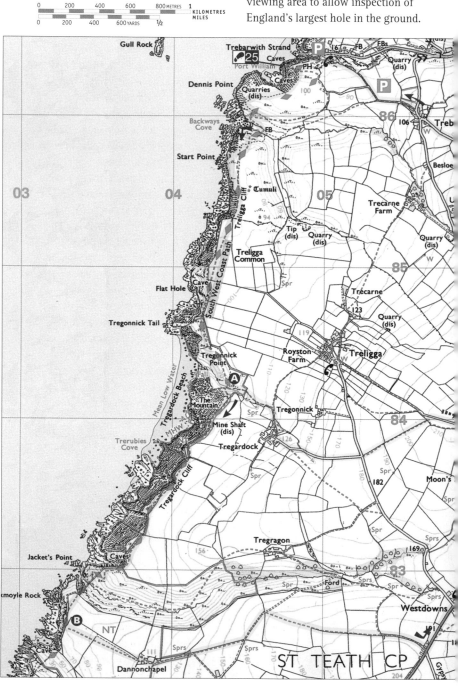

SCALE 1:25 000 or 2½ INCHES to 1 MILE 4CM to 1KM

Leave the quarry and follow the perimeter fence firstly past the fire station, and then the converted railway station on the left. Turn off to the left through new housing 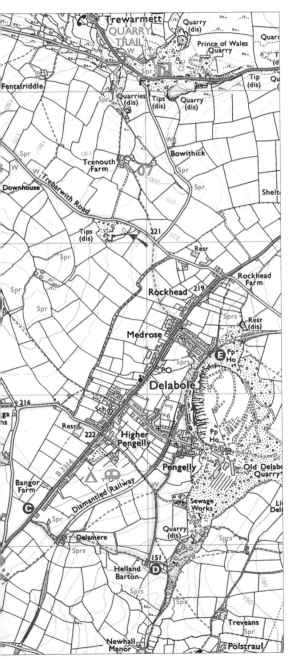 **E** to reach Medrose Street, and at the top turn right on to the main road. There is a footpath almost immediately on the left, before the Shell garage. This track is followed for a short distance before turning off to the right over a stone stile (before reaching the gate). Cross the meadow to another stone stile which takes the path over the next field. The following stile gives on to a very narrow meadow. Make your way across this to another stile and then walk across the field to the middle of the hedge on the right. Turn left on to the road.

This is a peaceful lane which sometimes allows wide views to the left to Port Isaac as it winds downhill, becoming steep as it approaches the hamlet of Trebarwith. The farm here is sadly derelict: pass it and take the footpath on the left which follows a track down through a meadow. The track becomes enclosed; continue to follow it, bearing right at the footpath junction, and then bear right again where the footpath divides once again. At some points the sunken track has become overgrown and the walking is easier above it. The way leads down to the side of Trebarwith valley, and then descends to rejoin the coastal footpath at Trebarwith Strand, the starting point.

Lamorna, St Loy's and the Merry Maidens

Start	Lamorna Cove
Distance	8½ miles (13.5km). Shorter version 5 miles (8km)
Approximate time	4 hours (2 hours for shorter version)
Parking	Lamorna Cove
Refreshments	Café on the quay at Lamorna Cove, Lamorna Wink pub is just off the main route
Ordnance Survey maps	Landranger 203 (Land's End) and Explorer 7 (Land's End)

This is a wonderful way to discover the great beauty of the Land's End peninsula. It seems to be a sad fact of life in the West Penwith district that a great many footpaths have been abandoned. The nearer one gets to Land's End, the worse the situation. Although the coastal path is well maintained, inland the story is very different. Fortunately the route described here survives, and is enjoyable for its inland sections (apart from the short length of road) just as much as the parts which follow the coastal path. In early spring the cliffs abound in daffodils and a little later with bluebells. If wished, a shorter version of the route can be taken, and the remaining section walked separately.

From the car park on the jetty at Lamorna take the coastal path south. Where the well-defined path peters out follow a yellow arrow uphill, scrambling over tumbled boulders. Easy stretches seem to alternate with difficult ones, where rocks have fallen from the cliff. Pass a small Celtic cross on Lamorna Point **Ⓐ**. Its inscription is badly weathered but appears to read *'Emma, March 13 1873'*. It is tempting to think that Emma was one of the young girls tragically drowned when the *Garonne* of Bordeaux was wrecked here in May, 1868. Her sixteen passengers included eight children, and the bodies of two young girls were subsequently washed up in the cove.

Soon the lighthouse at Tater-du comes into view and the way becomes less rugged. Dorminack, the farmhouse close to the path, was famous as the home of Derek Tangye. The lighthouse proves disappointingly unpicturesque close to. The path joins the drive to the lighthouse for a short distance before passing in front of cottages. From Boscawen Point, where a sort of logan-rock is perched, there is a glorious view to the west – one that is rarely seen in published photographs.

The path descends to the beach at St Loy's Cove **Ⓑ** which has to be crossed over great, rounded boulders. Take care here; it would be all too easy to twist or break an ankle. After this the

The Merry Maidens

About a mile (1.5km) of road follows, the only features of interest being an ancient cross and the remains of Tregiffian Barrow, a burial chamber of the 3rd millennium BC. Of more interest are the Merry Maidens **©** in a field on the right. Follow the footpath sign into this field and ponder on the fate of the Merry Maidens who according to legend were transmuted into stone for breaking the Sabbath. The two pipers who played for them to dance stand in adjoining fields on the opposite side of the road.

After examining the stone circle make for the far left-hand corner of the field where there is a stone stile in the hedge just before the gate. Cross this and the next field, making for a dead-end road sign. This cul-de-sac goes to Menwinnion Country Home for the Elderly and is the road which we take. As you walk along this lane you will glimpse the two stones known as The Pipers through the hedge on the left. Pass an old Wesleyan chapel on the right and fork left down towards Menwinnion. Where the lane bends again to the left, however, keep straight on down the footpath signposted to Lamorna, a lovely, though too short, part of the route. At the bottom turn right on to the road.

If you wish only to do the shorter version of the walk, continue down the road past the Lamorna Wink pub to the starting point at the jetty car park.

Take the lane which goes off to the left to Castallack, past the post office

path follows the course of a stream up its wooded valley; this section is steep with frequent zigzags along the way. At the top – which is actually a false summit – there is a stile, and beyond this the coastal footpath goes off to the left. Our route, however, lies to the right, continuing to follow the stream along its course.

Turn to the right to cross the stream following a sign on a sycamore tree. The path is jungly for a spell now, twisting by fuchsias, ferns, bamboos and hydrangeas intermingled with tree-high nettles. The stream is now close by on the left. The path becomes easier when it enters a wood, a delightfully cool section on a hot day. After a considerable distance it reaches the road through a white gate at the top. Turn right here.

SCALE 1:25 000 or 2½ INCHES to 1 MILE 4CM to 1KM

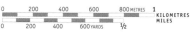

and Old Mill (unless you need refreshment, in which case continue down the road for a few yards to the pub). After passing the Old Mill look for a footpath on the right **D** at the end of a level stretch of lane. This is a pretty path up the side of the valley (though there is high bracken in places so be prepared for a soaking) with fine views down to the cove.

After a steep stone stile cross a field towards Kemyel Wartha. Pass through the farmyard to a path on the far side signposted to Mousehole. Keep to the

left of the first field and straight across the second. At the next head towards the right of the farm buildings. Pass the farmhouse on the left and go down the farm drive to a footpath sign on the right, at a gateway with a stone stile. Keep the hedge to the left at first but then cross a stone stile to reach a muddy stretch bridged at last by two large stones. The path winds through bracken and sloes to reach the farm track to Kemyel Drea. The path heads to the left of the farmhouse, passing through part of the farmyard by means of a series of stiles and finally a gate by a slurry tank; the ground here may be difficult to negotiate after wet weather.

At the end of the barn cross a stone stile to keep the hedge on your left, with a fine view of Mount's Bay ahead. There is a standing stone in this field and in the narrow one which follows. Strike diagonally across this field and climb the bank by stone steps about 20 yds (18m) from the bottom. Cross the next field diagonally to stone steps in much the same position as the previous ones. Descend to a gate giving on to a lane **E** (the coastal footpath) and turn right (unless you wish to explore Mousehole, in which case you turn left).

The track soon becomes a footpath passing above under-used allotments.

Hedges with fuchsias block the views, but these end suddenly as the path dips towards Slinke Dean and passes by a lookout post.

There is a short section where the path passes through unhealthy-looking pine trees by Slinke Dean. Then the path emerges on to the cliffside again, and there are wonderful coastal views.

From here the path is again strewn with boulders, as it was on the other side of Lamorna, and the walker is forced to make slow progress, scrambling at times. Almost too soon, though, the path reaches Lamorna where you can get excellent tea and cakes at the café. ●

Tintagel, Boscastle and St Nectan's Glen

Start	Tintagel
Distance	9 miles (14.5km)
Approximate time	5 hours
Parking	Car parks off Tintagel's main street
Refreshments	Cafés and pubs at Tintagel and Boscastle, tea-room at St Nectan's Glen
Ordnance Survey maps	Landrangers 190 (Bude & Clovelly) and 200 (Newquay & Bodmin) and Explorer 9 (Bodmin Moor)

The outward section of this walk uses a particularly spectacular stretch of the coastal footpath, and the walk would be worth doing for that alone; but we also have a lovely section through fields and the richly-wooded St Nectan's Glen, with its waterfall. As a bonus there is the opportunity of exploring a most beautiful fishing village. This is a strenuous walk, but very rewarding.

Both new and old post offices stand on the south-western side of the main street in Tintagel. Keep these on your left and make your way to the car park at the end of the street, where the path to the castle descends steeply down a rutted lane (there is a Land Rover service available for visitors not able to take exercise).

Walking down the main street of Tintagel one is almost overwhelmed by the gift shops selling souvenirs celebrating the Arthurian legend and left with a sense of foreboding that the castle and coastline will prove to be something of a let-down. However, few visitors will fail to recognise the romance of the place, which is perhaps best appreciated at a distance – away from the crowds. Our route bears to the right away from the castle beyond the café **Ⓐ**, and quite soon the throngs thin

out and one can sit and contemplate the great headland made famous by the inspiration of Tennyson. Even if you have earlier paid your money to English Heritage to visit the castle (the ruins you see are of a castle built in the twelfth century – nothing remains of Arthur's stronghold, if there ever was one) it is best to savour the place from near the opposing headland, Barras Nose. This is famous for its gloomy cave, well seen from the coast path. It must have been one of the National Trust's first properties, having been acquired in 1896.

The next headland is, if possible, even more memorable. This is Willapark **Ⓑ**, not to be confused with another Willapark which overlooks Boscastle harbour – the National Trust write the second one Willa Park. As the path drops to Bossiney one cannot avoid noticing the ranks of caravans drawn up on the cliff top, both on the right and ahead. The descent to Bossiney can be difficult if wet, though there are steps on the other side to help with the climb.

The view ahead is now of a succession of magnificent headlands, with seas beating against their precipitous flanks and pouring off rocky ledges. The sound is as marvellous as the sight: think of the terrible plight of those wrecked off this shore in days gone by. Pause before the descent to Rocky Valley **C** to notice how the scenery becomes even more rugged beyond, especially with the jagged spires of rock off Trevalga Cliff.

Ladies Window

Rocky Valley itself is delightful, fully living up to its name. Small waterfalls and swirlholes interrupt the sparkling progress of the little stream, which flows through a narrow glen-like valley (appropriately, for this is the seaward end of St Nectan's Glen). The climb back up to the clifftop is quite severe.

Firebeacon Hill is notable for a pinnacle of rock on its western side and for the remarkable formation known as the Ladies Window **D** which is best seen from the seat at the top.

After yet another descent and ascent at Welltown, the path approaches the next great headland – Willapark, which has a murky zawn (a sea cave aptly named Western Blackapit) at its base. Here **E** there is a choice of route. If you are already familiar with Boscastle and wish to avoid the steep climb out of the village, bear off to the right to the church and then head for Paradise (really – see the map).

The more usual way will be to visit the picturesque little village of Boscastle, dropping to the southern side of the quay. Having explored the village's attractions, cross the main road to the lane by the Wellington

Hotel and climb up steeply, forking left to pass the post office. Cross straight over the main road to reach Paradise, a lovely street of old houses including the famous Napoleon Inn which dates from the 16th century; a century or so ago, when the fortunes of the harbour were at their zenith, the village had eighteen alehouses. Turn right at the crossroads to follow a level lane and, where this turns up to the right to join the main road, take the farm track on the left **F**. There is a fine view of the village from here.

After a Z-bend look for a stone stile on the right and cross two fields, making for another stile in the top corner of the second one. Keep on the left side of the first part of the next field, following the waymark to cut across the top of it.

Turn left out of the gateway to stone steps up a bank. Strike across this field to a gate at the top right-hand corner (the waymark points along the hedge here but is incorrect). Turn left on to a farm track and follow it to the road where you bear right. Just after the driveway to Trehane Farm turn left into a farm track and look immediately for a

SCALE 1:25 000 or 2½ INCHES to 1 MILE 4CM to 1KM

```
0    200   400   600   800 METRES  1
                                    KILOMETRES
                                    MILES
0    200   400   600 YARDS   ½
```

stone stile on the right. Cross the field diagonally to a gate at the bottom-right corner and turn left into a lane.

The lane winds down past Tredole Farm almost to the bottom of the valley but just before this there is a very-concealed stile in the hedge on the right **G**. Climb this to cross two narrow fields (there may be mushrooms here). At the far side of the second field there is a stile and a footbridge to cross. Keep the ditch on the left and cross the

stream by another footbridge. The path follows the left bank of the stream through the next meadow where the path divides.

We cross the stream again to follow its right bank towards St Nectan's Glen. Climb up to a stile by a rocky outcrop where it looks as though the obvious route passes by a ruined barn. The barn is subsequently reached by a descent down a sunken lane. The path now leads into the glen itself, passing the site of the old Hermitage tea-garden **H**, now abandoned. As the path continues through the wood the sound of the

waterfall is tantalising, but it cannot be glimpsed. It must have been a damp home for a hermit here.

The path crosses over the stream twice, first by way of a a wooden footbridge, then via a concrete one. At the third footbridge, turn left to cross it and follow the path to Halgabron up the side of the valley. Pass out of the glen at the top through a kissing-gate. Go straight across the meadow to reach a stone stile on the far side. Turn left into a lane and after 200 yds (184m) take a footpath to the right which crosses a field. Keep the hedge on the right to reach a stone stile by a farmhouse.

Turn to the right down the road (this road becomes very busy in the summer: take care when walking it) and when it bends to the right take the footpath signposted on the left, crossing the field diagonally to a gate situated in the bottom right-hand corner. Maintain the same course over the next field to find a stile in front of a greywashed house. The road is reached just to the right of this house. Turn left along the road which leads to the centre of Tintagel and the starting point. ●

The Dodman, Gorran Haven and Portmellon

The Dodman, Gorran Haven and Portmellon

Start	Caerhays (Porthluney) beach, south-west of Mevagissey
Distance	11 miles (17.5km). Shorter version 7½ miles (12km)
Approximate time	6 hours (4 hours for shorter version)
Parking	Car park at Caerhays (Porthluney) beach
Refreshments	Cafés at Caerhays, Gorran Haven and Portmellon in season, pubs at Gorran Haven, Portmellon and Gorran Churchtown
Ordnance Survey maps	Landranger 204 (Truro & Falmouth), Pathfinder 1361, SW 94/SX 04 (Mevagissey & Tregony)

This walk proves that it is a mistake to consider the south coast easy walking in comparison with the north. It is a strenuous all-day excursion, which embraces some of the finest cliff scenery in England. Fortunately the lovely return through woods, fields and lanes is less demanding both of time and effort, and this makes it one of Cornwall's classic walks. If wished, a shorter version of the walk can be taken, missing Portmellon.

Leave the car park by the exit on to the road and turn right to cross the bridge which, like the perimeter wall of the castle (by John Nash, completed 1808), is castellated. Take the coastal footpath which climbs the eastern side of the beach, a hard enough gradient to start with but good practice for what is to come. The reward is a fine view of the castle and its grounds.

The footpath still demands energy as it descends to Lambsowden Cove, but it is well maintained and the scenery is exceptional – this is not a crowded part of the South Coast Way. There is a steep ascent to Greeb Point and then a relatively level stretch before the descent to lovely Hemmick Beach **Ⓐ**.

Greeb Point was the scene of a 'Brandy Galore' episode in January

1838 when the aptly-named brig *Brandywine Packet* became embayed by a strong gale and eventually struck here. The one survivor managed to scramble on to Gwineas Rock and was later rescued by the revenue cutter. Three to four hundred barrels of the *Brandywine*'s cargo were washed ashore and the villagers made ready for a party, but the revenue men were too quick for them and nearly all were recovered intact.

The climb on the other side of Hemmick is the start of the 374-ft (114m) assault on the Dodman, though disconcertingly after a climb of 100ft (30m) or so the path descends to Gell Point. The view from here is truly stupendous – the telecommunication dishes at Goonhilly being ubiquitous landmarks, about the only man-made objects to be seen. Keep to the coastal path where the choice is offered at Collars Road. The giant cross erected in 1896 on the Dodman **B** can now clearly be seen ahead.

Veryan Bay

Now that the point is rounded Bow Beach is seen below and St Austell Bay beyond. To landward the top of the tower of Gorran church appears, with white spoil heaps of china clay behind. The hedgerows here have the plumpest sloes you are ever likely to see, though if you are here in early summer the abundance of wild flowers will more than recompense.

The National Trust owns the Lamledra property here, and the path descends through it to Bow Beach, then climbs again to reach Maenease Point. After this it is little distance to the ice creams, tea and beer awaiting at Gorran Haven **C**.

At this point, those wishing only to do the shorter version of the walk can take the road climbing through the village to Gorran Churchtown, rejoining the main route there.

The pub is at the northern end of the village. Before you reach it bear right just beyond Mount Zion church, past Rose Cottage. Then bear right again at the Cliff Road roadsign for Portmellon. At Perhaver cross the stone stile to a proper cliff path.

The white houses on Chapel Point are soon up ahead as the path rounds Turbot Point and now Mevagissey is in view. A metalled road takes walkers down to Portmellon **D**.

Here there are several choices. Portmellon has an excellent pub, the Rising Sun, which can be recommended as a good place to consider them. Mevagissey is not far from here, and if energy permits can be explored. The official footpath from Portmellon to Gorran Churchtown follows the north side of the valley, but to reach it one has to climb up through new housing. Locals say that there is a definitive path to Galowras Mill along the south side of the valley which is most attractive; this is reached through the boatyard, but is not marked on the map. We take the official route, which is only marred by the ten-minute haul up through the new estate.

From the Rising Sun turn right on to the seafront and then right again up a new road, passing regimented bungalows each with a wrought-iron terrace above a double garage. Climb to the top of this development to find a signpost and farm track on the left to Penwarne Farm. Go through the farmyard, with the farmhouse on the left, to a blue gate. Keep the wall on the left, now, as the path follows the right flank of the valley along the contours. This pleasant path makes up for the new housing. When another valley joins from the right descend across it to

a gate. This leads to Galowras Mill **E**.
Bear left across the bridge away from
the house and climb up the drive to the
first bend to a footpath sign to
St Gorran's Church on the right. There
is also a notice saying that this is West
Bodrugan Wood Nature Reserve and
requesting people to walk quietly, with
dogs on leads. This is a lovely part of
the route, though steep at times and not
well waymarked. When you are faced
by an iron gate in front and a cattle
shelter on the left at the end of the
wood, turn right downhill to find a stile
into a meadow.

Pass a lovely group of trees, an ash
and three very ancient oaks, to reach a
gate by a stream at the bottom of the
field. Go through the gate and climb to
a stile by a solitary oak. Now climb the
steep hill keeping to the right of the
fence. At the top cross the stone stile
and then the field to another stone stile
to the left of the building on the right.
Gorran church is now ahead. Make
directly for it, crossing two more stone
stiles to reach a lane. Turn left to reach
the church and pub **F**.

Gorran church is everything an
English parish church ought to be,
especially when seen dressed overall for
its harvest festival. It is a shining
testament to 2000 years of faith. Note
the wonderfully-carved bench ends and
the famous brass to the Lady of Branall
who died in 1510.

Leave the churchyard at its western
end and walk up past the Barley Sheaf
pub. Turn left at the post office to
Treveor. This path is easy to follow.
Note many of the stiles along the way
have used old stone field-rollers for
their top bars. Cross one lane, turn left
towards Treveor Farm at the second,
and bear to the right at the road
junction. Beyond the farm, where there
is coarse fishing in the ponds, glimpses
of the sea appear ahead.

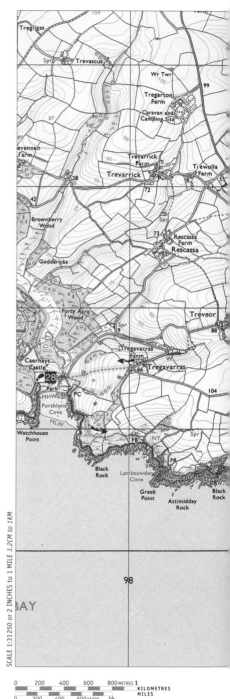

SCALE 1:31250 or 2 INCHES to 1 MILE 3.2CM to 1KM

As the lane begins to descend more
steeply, and before it turns sharply
right, take the footpath on the left to

Tregavarras. Descend to the bottom of the field (well to the left of the buildings) to a bridge and stile, and then cross the stepping-stones to pass the houses and so reach the lane. Turn right at Tregavarras, by an old ivy-clad cottage where the road bends sharply left, on to the path to Caerhays. This is a lovely end to a fine walk: there are splendid views of the castle and lake, and of Veryan Bay, before the path descends to the bridge and car park. ●

Further Information

The National Trust

Anyone who likes visiting places of natural beauty and/or historic interest has cause to be grateful to the National Trust. Without it, many such places would probably have vanished by now. It was in response to the pressures on the countryside posed by the relentless march of Victorian industrialisation that the trust was set up in 1895. Its founders, inspired by the common goals of protecting and conserving Britain's national heritage and widening public access to it, were Sir Robert Hunter, Octavia Hill and Canon Rawnsley: respectively a solicitor, a social reformer and a clergyman. The latter was particularly influential. As a canon of Carlisle Cathedral and vicar of Crosthwaite (near Keswick), he was concerned about threats to the Lake District and had already been active in protecting footpaths and promoting public access to open countryside. After the flooding of Thirlmere in 1879 to create a large reservoir, he became increasingly convinced that the only effective way to guarantee protection was outright ownership of land.

The purpose of the National Trust is to preserve areas of natural beauty and sites of historic interest by acquisition, holding them in trust for the nation and making them available for public enjoyment. Some of its properties have been acquired through purchase, but many have been donated. Nowadays it is not only one of the biggest landowners in the country, but also one of the most active conservation charities, protecting 581,113 acres (253,176 ha) of land, including 555 miles (892km) of coastline, and over 300 historic properties in England, Wales and Northern Ireland. (There is a separate National Trust for Scotland, which was set up in 1931.)

Furthermore, once a piece of land has come under National Trust ownership, it is difficult for its status to be altered. As a result of parliamentary legislation in 1907, the Trust was given the right to declare its property inalienable, so ensuring that in any subsequent dispute it can appeal directly to parliament.

As it works towards its dual aims of conserving areas of attractive countryside and encouraging greater public access (not easy to reconcile in this age of mass tourism), the Trust provides an excellent service for walkers by creating new concessionary paths and waymarked trails, maintaining stiles and foot bridges and combating the ever-increasing problem of footpath erosion.

In Cornwall, the National Trust offers something for everyone: sandy beaches, coastal walks, spring gardens and country houses. The county is particularly fortunate in having a greater proportion of its beautiful stretches of coast and countryside protected by the Trust than any other county in Britain. Wherever you roam in the county you are likely to encounter the familiar metal oak leaf sign indicating that the landscape in which you walk is protected forever.

About $\frac{1}{3}$ of Cornwall's coastline is owned by the National Trust under the colourful banner of its Enterprise Neptune appeal which aims to protect the unspoilt coastline of England, Wales and Northern Ireland. Highlights in Cornwall include Sandymouth, Holywell and Crantock beaches, headlands such as Nare Head and The Dodman, stunning Cape Cornwall given to the Trust by H.J. Heinz and last, but by no means least, the fairytale castle of St Michael's Mount perched on its rocky crag in Mount's Bay.

If gardening is your hobby there is much to enjoy at the gardens the Trust cares for in Cornwall. The mild climate encourages the growth of many plants and shrubs which do not normally flourish elsewhere, and the display of spring blooms is quite magnificent.

The various periods of architecture and furnishings in country houses are well represented in the Trust's Cornish properties, from medieval and Tudor Cotehele through Elizabethan Trerice, eighteenth-century Antony House and on to the high Victorian style of the rebuilt parts of Lanhydrock – the great house of Cornwall.

If you would like more information about the National Trust, or would like to purchase leaflets from a series which covers the coastal properties owned by the Trust in Cornwall, please contact the Regional Office at the address on page 95. For details of membership, contact the membership department at the address on the same page.

■ Walkers and the Law

The average walker in a national park or other popular walking area, armed with the appropriate Ordnance Survey map, reinforced perhaps by a guidebook giving detailed walking instructions, is unlikely to run into legal difficulties, but it is useful to know something about the law relating to public rights of way. The right to walk over certain parts of the countryside has developed over a long period, and how such rights came into being is a complex subject, too lengthy to be discussed here. The following comments are intended simply as a helpful guide, backed up by the Countryside Access Charter, a concise summary of walkers' rights and obligations drawn up by the Countryside Commission.

Basically there are two main kinds of public rights of way: footpaths (for walkers only) and bridleways (for walkers, riders on horseback and pedal cyclists). Footpaths and bridleways are shown by broken green lines on Ordnance Survey Pathfinder and

Outdoor Leisure maps and broken red lines on Landranger maps. There is also a third category, called byways: chiefly broad tracks (green lanes) or farm roads, which walkers, riders and cyclists have to share, usually only occasionally, with motor vehicles. Many of these public paths have been in existence for hundreds of years and some even originated as prehistoric trackways and have been in constant use for well over 2000 years. Ways known as RUPPs (roads used as public paths) still appear on some maps. The legal definition of such byways is ambiguous and they are gradually being reclassified as footpaths, bridleways or byways.

The term 'right of way' means exactly what it says. It gives right of passage over what, in the vast majority of cases, is private land, and you are required to keep to the line of the path and not stray on to the land on either side. If you inadvertently wander off the right of way – either because of faulty map-reading or because the route is not clearly indicated on the ground – you are technically trespassing and the wisest course is to ask the nearest available person (farmer or fellow walker) to direct you back to the correct route. There are stories about unpleasant confrontations between walkers and farmers at times, but in general most farmers are co-operative when responding to a

Boscastle

Further Information

genuine and polite request for assistance in route-finding.

Obstructions can sometimes be a problem and probably the most common of these is where a path across a field has been ploughed up. It is legal for a farmer to plough up a path provided that he restores it within two weeks, barring exceptionally bad weather. This does not always happen and here the walker is presented with a dilemma: to follow the line of the path, even if this inevitably means treading on crops, or to walk around the edge of the field. The latter course of action often seems the best but this means that you would be trespassing and not keeping to the exact line of the path. In the case of other obstructions which may block a path (illegal fences and locked gates etc), common sense has to be used in order to negotiate them by the easiest method – detour or removal. You should only ever remove as much as is necessary to get through, and if you can easily go round the obstruction without causing any damage, then you should do so. If you have any problems negotiating rights of way, you should report the matter to the rights of way department of the relevant council, which will take action with the landowner concerned.

Apart from rights of way enshrined by law, there are a number of other paths available to walkers. Permissive or concessionary paths have been created where a landowner has allowed the public to use a particular route across his land. The main problem with these is that, as they have been granted as a concession, there is no legal right to use them and therefore they can be closed at any time. In practice, many of these concessionary routes have been established on land owned either by large public bodies such as the Forestry Commission, or by a private one, such as the National Trust, and as these mainly encourage walkers to use their paths, they are unlikely to be closed unless a change of ownership occurs.

Walkers also have free access to country parks (except where requested to keep away from certain areas for ecological reasons, eg. wildlife protection, woodland regeneration, safeguarding of rare plants etc), canal towpaths and most beaches. By custom, though not by right, you are generally free to walk across the open and uncultivated higher land of mountain, moorland and fell, but this varies from area to area and from one season to another – grouse moors, for example, will be out of bounds during the breeding and shooting seasons and some open areas are used as Ministry of Defence firing ranges, for which reason access will be restricted. In some areas the situation has been clarified as a result of 'access agreements' between the landowners and either the county council or the national park authority, which clearly define when and where you can walk over such open country.

■ The Ramblers' Association

No organisation works more actively to protect and extend the rights and interests of walkers in the countryside than the Ramblers' Association. Its aims are clear: to foster a greater knowledge, love and care of the countryside; to assist in the protection and enhancement of public rights of way and areas of natural beauty; to work for greater public access to the countryside; and to encourage more people to take up rambling as a healthy, recreational leisure activity.

It was founded in 1935 when, following the setting up of a National Council of Ramblers' Federations in 1931, a number of federations earlier formed in London, Manchester, the Midlands and elsewhere came together to create a more effective pressure group, to deal with such problems as the disappearance and obstruction of footpaths, the prevention of access to open mountain and moorland and

Countryside Access Charter

Your rights of way are:

- public footpaths – on foot only. Sometimes waymarked in yellow
- bridleways – on foot, horseback and pedal cycle. Sometimes waymarked in blue
- byways (usually old roads), most 'roads used as public paths' and, of course, public roads – all traffic has the right of way

Use maps, signs and waymarks to check rights of way. Ordnance Survey Pathfinder and Landranger maps show most public rights of way

On rights of way you can:

- take a pram, pushchair or wheelchair if practicable
- take a dog (on a lead or under close control)
- take a short route round an illegal obstruction or remove it sufficiently to get past

You have a right to go for recreation to:

- public parks and open spaces – on foot
- most commons near older towns and cities – on foot and sometimes on horseback
- private land where the owner has a formal agreement with the local authority

In addition you can use the following by local or established custom or consent, but ask for advice if you are unsure:

- many areas of open country, such as moorland, fell and coastal areas, especially those in the care of the National Trust, and some commons
- some woods and forests, especially those owned by the Forestry Commission
- country parks and picnic sites
- most beaches
- canal towpaths
- some private paths and tracks Consent sometimes extends to horse-riding and cycling

For your information:

- county councils and London boroughs maintain and record rights of way, and register commons
- obstructions, dangerous animals, harassment and misleading signs on rights of way are illegal and you should report them to the county council
- paths across fields can be ploughed, but must normally be reinstated within two weeks
- landowners can require you to leave land to which you have no right of access
- motor vehicles are normally permitted only on roads, byways and some 'roads used as public paths'

---

increasing hostility from landowners. This was the era of the mass trespasses, when there were sometimes violent confrontations between ramblers and gamekeepers, especially on the moorlands of the Peak District.

Since then the Ramblers' Association has played an influential role in preserving and developing the national footpath network, supporting the creation of national parks and encouraging the designation and waymarking of long-distance routes.

Our freedom to walk in the countryside is precarious and requires constant vigilance. As well as the perennial problems of footpaths being illegally obstructed, disappearing

through lack of use or extinguished by housing or road construction, new dangers can spring up at any time.

It is to meet such problems and dangers that the Ramblers' Association exists and represents the interests of all walkers. The address to write to for information on the Ramblers' Association and how to become a member is given on page 95.

Walking Safety

The cliffs and moors of Cornwall, though they may look innocuous enough in good weather, need to be treated with respect. They can quickly be transformed into wet, misty, gale-torn and potentially dangerous areas of wilderness in bad weather. Even on an outwardly fine and settled summer day, conditions can rapidly deteriorate. In winter, of course, the weather is even more untrustworthy and the hours of daylight much shorter.

Therefore it is advisable to always take both warm and waterproof clothing, sufficient nourishing food, a hot drink, first-aid kit, torch and whistle. Wear suitable footwear, ie. strong walking boots or shoes that give a good grip over rocky terrain and on slippery slopes. Try to obtain a local weather forecast and bear it in mind before you start. Do not be afraid to abandon your proposed route and return to your starting point in the event of a sudden and unexpected deterioration in the weather. Do not go alone and allow enough time to finish the walk well before nightfall.

Most of the walks described in this book will be safe to do, given due care and respect, at any time of year in all but the most unreasonable weather. Indeed, a crisp, fine winter day often

Kynance Cove

provides perfect walking conditions, with firm ground underfoot and a clarity that is not possible to achieve in the other seasons of the year. A few of the walks, however, are suitable only for reasonably fit and experienced walkers and should definitely not be tackled by anyone else during the winter months or in bad weather, especially high winds and mist. These are indicated in the general description that precedes each of the walks.

Useful Organisations

Council for the Protection of Rural England
Warwick House, 25 Buckingham Palace Road, London SW1W 0PP
Tel. 0171 976 6433
Countryside Commission
John Dower House, Crescent Place, Cheltenham, Gloucestershire GL50 3RA
Tel. 01242 521381
Forestry Commission
Information Department, 231 Corstorphine Road, Edinburgh EH12 7AT
Tel. 0131 334 0303

Long Distance Walkers' Association
21 Upcroft, Windsor,
Berkshire SL4 3NH
Tel. 01753 866685

National Trust
Membership and general enquiries:
PO Box 39, Bromley, Kent BR1 3XL
Tel. 0181 315 1111
Cornwall regional office:
Lanhydrock, Bodmin, PL30 4DE
Tel. 01208 74281

Ordnance Survey
Romsey Road, Maybush, Southampton
SO16 4GU
Tel. 08456 05 05 05 (Lo-call)

Ramblers' Association
1/5 Wandsworth Road, London
SW8 2XX
Tel. 0171 582 6878

Local contact *(in case of obstructions or
other problems)*
Shirley Oliver (Secretary),
Trenoweth, Viaduct Hill, Hayle,
Cornwall TR27 5HT
Tel. 01736 752121

West Country Tourist Board
60, St David's Hill, Exeter, Devon
EX4 4SY
Tel. 01392 76351

Cornwall Tourist Board
59 Lemon Street, Truro TR1 2SY
Tel. 01872 74057
Local tourist information offices:
Bude: 01288 354240
Camelford: 01840 212954
Falmouth: 01326 312300
Fowey: 01726 833616
Helston & Lizard Peninsula:
 01326 565431
Launceston: 01566 772321/772333
Looe: 01503 262072
Newquay: 01637 871345
Padstow: 01841 533449
Penzance: 01736 62207
Plymouth: 01752 264849
St Ives: 01736 796297
Isles of Scilly: 01720 422536
Truro: 01872 74555

Youth Hostels Association
Trevelyan House, 8 St Stephen's Hill, St
Albans, Hertfordshire AL1 2DY
Tel. 01727 855215

 ## Ordnance Survey Maps of Cornwall

Cornwall is covered by Ordnance
Survey 1:50 000 scale ($1\frac{1}{4}$ inches to
1 mile or 2cm to 1km) Landranger map
sheets 190, 200, 201, 203 and 204.
 These all-purpose maps are packed
with information to help you explore
the area. Viewpoints, picnic sites, places
of interest and caravan and camping
sites, are shown as well as public rights
of way information such as footpaths
and bridleways.
 To examine Cornwall in more detail
and especially if you are planning
walks, the Ordnance Survey Pathfinder
maps at 1:25 000 scale ($2\frac{1}{2}$ inches to
1 mile or 4cm to 1km) are ideal. Maps
covering the area are:

1273 (SS 21/31)	1352 (SW 75)
1292 (SS 20/30)	1353 (SW 85/95)
1310 (SX 19)	1354 (SX 05/15)
1311 (SX 29/39)	1355 (SW 25/35)
1326 (SX 28/38)	1356 (SZ 45/55)
1337 (SW 87/97)	1359 (SW 54/64)
1339 (SX 27/37)	1360 (SW 74/84)
1346 (SW 86/96)	1361 (SW 94/SX04)
1347 (SX 06/16)	1365 (SW 63/53/73)
1348 (SX 26/36)	1366 (SW 83/73/93)

Explorer maps available in this area are
No. 7 (Land's End), No. 8 (The Lizard),
and No. 9 (Bodmin Moor). Tourists will
also find the Touring Map and Guide
No. 13, *Devon and Cornwall* useful, as it
provides lots of information on where
to go and what to see.
 To get to Cornwall use the Ordnance
Survey Great Britain Routeplanner,
Travelmaster map number 1, at
1:625 000 (1 inch to 10 miles or 4cm to
25km) scale.
 Ordnance Survey maps and guides
are available from most booksellers,
stationers and newsagents.

Index

Entries in italics refer to illustrations